Spontaneous Human Combustion

The True Story of How One Christian
Woman Found Explosive Love.

LIV DIETRICH

WESTBOW
PRESS
A DIVISION OF THOMAS NELSON
& ZONDERVAN

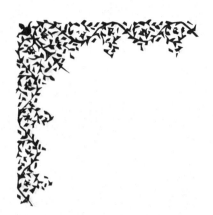

WestBow Press books may be ordered through booksellers or by contacting:

WestBow Press
A Division of Thomas Nelson & Zondervan
1663 Liberty Drive
Bloomington, IN 47403
www.westbowpress.com
1 (866) 928-1240

ISBN: 978-1-4908-6825-7 (sc)
ISBN: 978-1-4908-6824-0 (e)

Library of Congress Control Number: 2015901390

Print information available on the last page.

WestBow Press rev. date: 02/26/2015

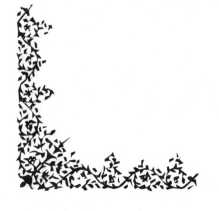

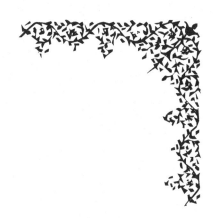

This is a completely factual story. Only the names, places and dates of two events have been changed. Those changes were made to protect the guilty, the innocent and those that don't know in which category they belong.

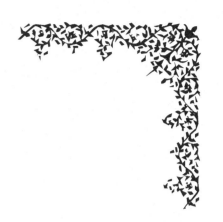

"Spontaneous human combustion" refers to the destruction of the flesh by internal fire originating without an apparent external source of ignition.

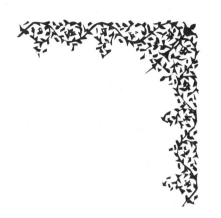

I had received no communication from my high-school sweetheart for thirty-five years. Then, one sunny, cold January afternoon, while innocently surfing the Net, I saw his name and city on Classmates.com. There it was—Jaziel Bachman, Winnipeg, Manitoba—right on the screen in front of me, Alexa Coljen, Rome, New York. My heart shifted into high gear. Suddenly, there was hope that my life would change from happily living in misery to happily living in happiness.

As I sat in my office on my turquoise leather-tufted CEO chair, I looked out my window at the deep snow. The hills, evergreens, and the two-lane road were blanketed in white. It was much too cold to even think about opening some other real estate broker's frozen lock box. I didn't want to traipse up a listing's unshoveled driveway just to freeze my fingers. Houses had not been selling.

Better to look online for hot apple pie recipes, warm leather fashion boots, and stylish woolen jackets. I certainly did not want to browse any depressing national or world news. That would have been like placing an elephant's foot on my chest and I certainly didn't need to be pressed down more than I already was. Then an innocent pop-up ad appeared: "WONDER WHERE YOUR CLASSMATES ARE NOW? CLICK HERE to FIND OUT." I wondered what changes thirty-five years had made to Jaz Bachman. Did he even believe in God?

There's nothing in the Bible about finding high-school sweethearts online. I had only seen his name. That's innocent, isn't it? Then I sent one brief e-mail to him to confirm that he was the same Jaziel Bachman. It was not even remotely likely that somebody else with that name would be listed as an alumnus of the year he graduated, the year before me. Did I even dare to allow myself to have these irrational feelings? My heart was beating very fast. Did somebody turn the thermostat way up in my office?

How was something going to happen? He lived two thousand miles away. I had a good Christian life, as far as anybody could tell. It would take some kind of a

miracle, either one I made up or one God actually made. When did he move to Winnipeg? A lot of life had happened in the past thirty-five years. Come to think about it, more than a few times, that life was near death.

Jaz and I had enjoyed an innocent, storybook relationship in high school. Picnics on a blanket. Movies at the drive-in theatre. Pizza at Papa Roma's. Canoe trips with our group of friends. He had adored my long, dark hair and I had liked his long, blond curls. He had a pleasingly white smile and ocean-blue eyes.

Then he had graduated, his family moving to Toronto, far away from our high school, and the relationship had ended. There was no Internet back then. I had told my mother to tell him that I wasn't home when he called.

One year later, he had ridden his motorcycle all the way back to our high school and appeared near my locker, wearing a gray leather jacket and carrying two helmets. He had said he wanted me to get onto the back of the bike and ride to Toronto with him, leaving home forever. I had told him no. I had already made plans to go to the senior picnic and I didn't want to miss that!

I am now living in a huge lodge—Coljens Lodge—that I use about once a month on weekends for Christian women's retreats for a hundred women. It is about half a mile from Coljens Realty. My ex-husband and I have four grown-up-and-out kids. Technically, they were artificially conceived, since the marriage certainly had been artificial. Now I was officially alone. It really was an empty nest. With nine fold-out couches, thirteen beds, and various other empty sleeping places, it was sort of a lodge full of empty nests. I was still staying in the lodge, just like the rest of the furniture. The furniture was ready to go but I wasn't. What kind of a life would I have?

I remembered how God had healed me of a fatal blood disease two years after high-school graduation. I had been living in the sorority at the university. They had found me lying in my walk-in closet and had to transport me by ambulance to the hospital. I was in a semi-coma, with a blood count of two. Twelve to fifteen is normal. I had looked like a skeleton.

I had been an outpatient for a year, with many blood draws and tests. I had had my blood drawn so frequently that my veins were scarred and it was hard for the technicians to use the needle for more draws. There was no cure. After three weeks in the hospital room, Dorothy, my friend since fourth grade, had come, wearing her Salvation Army uniform, and had prayed for me.

The day after Dorothy prayed, I sat up in the hospital bed with a bewildered look on my face. The last thing I remembered was sitting on the floor of my closet in the sorority.

The quite muscular nurse barked, "You're almost dead! Lie down!"

I replied in a strong and stable voice, "If I'm almost dead, you better call a code blue."

She ran out of the room.

That works just like on TV. I put my feet on the floor, pulled the IV out of my wrist, scurried over to the locker, grabbed my very baggy bellbottoms off the hook and pulled my baggy T-shirt over my hospital gown. I tucked it into my jeans, slipped on my chunky heeled sandals, and exited before Nurse Onsteroids or anybody else could get back to my room. I easily walked two miles to my university apartment, holding my jeans up with thumbs through the belt loops.

If God had healed me like that, He could do anything. He could even put Jaz and me back together. That would be a miracle.

The information on Classmates.com said that Jaziel Bachman was a high-school music teacher. He had three grown children. I wasn't sure that was true. How could he have married somebody when he surely loved *me?* That's what he had said when we were in high school. Everything online may not be true. Classmates.com had listed my city incorrectly. They had it as Rome, Italy, but it was really Rome, New York. I wasn't sure what to hope.

Anyway, I didn't dare tell any of my Christian friends that I was suddenly head-over-heels over somebody with whom I hadn't communicated in thirty-five years. They would reiterate that Christian women were supposed to have stayed married and should have acted like the Proverbs 31 wife. They would say that Christians aren't supposed to look online for high-school sweethearts after their divorces or maybe any other time.

Maybe there is supposed to be some socially acceptable mourning period after a divorce. Even if the screen flashes, "CLICK HERE," Christian women aren't supposed to click. Christian women are supposed to focus on God and act like Mother Teresa or somebody similar.

The same day that I clicked Jaz's name, in the middle of the night, I was sleeping peacefully under my fluffy navy blue quilt. Then something even more exciting than finding Jaz Bachman happened. I was awakened by the sound of music! It

was not the musical with Julie Andrews, but the sound of real music. It sounded like an explosion shooting whistling streams of red fire into my dark room, except it had a melody and words. I jumped out of bed and saw that there wasn't any fire in the bedroom ... as usual.

That first night that the explosion happened, I stood there looking around, wondering if somebody had installed some loudspeakers in my bedroom. Nobody was in the room but me. No loudspeakers. The combusting music was inside me! I had heard of spontaneous human combustion. My heart was ticking like a bomb about to explode! This was amazing! I wondered if all that was going to be left of me would be a little pile of ashes.

As long as I was out of bed, I figured I might as well visit my bathroom. The master bathroom was beautiful. I had custom-ordered the two-person navy whirlpool tub, the matching navy double sinks set into knotty aspen cabinetry and the large white ceramic tiles covering the floor and running halfway up the walls. The tiles looked like soft white clouds.

I decided to write down what I had heard on some tissues from a box on the bathroom counter. I used a black eyeliner pencil since there weren't any pens handy. This is what I wrote:

1/2/2007
(heavy rock music)

Innocence

God forgives with innocence
God forgives with innocence
He puts us back
To where we were
And it's as if
No sin occurred
God forgives with innocence
God forgives with innocence
Heals us with
His Holy Word
And it's as if

No sin occurred
He takes away
The sin and shame
He forgives
And there's no blame
God forgives with innocence
God forgives with innocence
Innocence
Innocence
Innocence
Yah!

The next night, not expecting this to be a nightly occurrence, I wrote with the black eyeliner on the back of a church bulletin that I had left on the double-sink counter. I woke up hearing the words, rushed over to the bathroom, sat on the tiled whirlpool step and wrote them down as I heard them.

1/3/2007 3 am

Luke 12:22–31 NIV "... do not worry about your life ... seek his kingdom, and these things will be given to you as well."
(About not seeking material things, only seek the giving Spirit of God.)
(God speaking)

Giving

It is my desire
To give freely to all men
To give life, love, happiness
Joy complete within

And when I see the raven
The lowliest of birds
My heart is filled with kindness
With more than only words

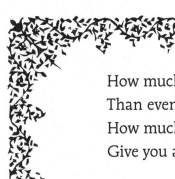

How much more I love you
Than even such as these
How much more I want to
Give you all I please

Find me with your whole heart
My love, my joy, my peace
In my great provision
Will be your great relief.

In the morning, I observed that the design of my headboard included tall cabinets on both sides, but no writing surface. No problem. I put some lined paper, left behind by one of the kids, next to the whirlpool tub in the master bath. I could hop out of bed and use the tiled ledge around the blue tub for a writing surface. I could sit on the tiled step and the paper could fit on the ledge. I put a pen there, too. I was thinking about Jaz Bachman. I wondered what his house looked like.

After about a week of sitting on the cold tiled step in the middle of the night, I decided to try to make it all the way down to my home office desk to write down what I heard. I kept my fuzzy blue bed socks on and put my bright red fake fur robe at the foot of the bed. The master bedroom was thirty by thirty feet, with the bed opposite the door. By the time I slid on the waxed wood floor to the bedroom door, scurried across the adjoining sitting loft, slipped down the wood stairs, crossed the slate lobby, crossed the three story great room, pushed the spindle chairs to get through the dining hall, stepped carefully so as not to slip on the granite kitchen floor, not banging into the counters in the dark, passed the fern patterned guest bath, and slid quickly down the long pantry hall to my home office, I forgot the words.

That was no problem though, because God just woke me up again with the same song explosion a couple hours after I fell asleep again. I decided to stick with just slip-sliding to the whirlpool tub. This went on for a couple more weeks. Soon I had a package of lined paper, pens, my Bible, various sizes of notebooks, my red robe, bottles of orange juice, pecan cookies, and some Pez candy dispensers all in the whirlpool tub.

God usually woke me up with the first couple of lines and then waited until I slid over to the whirlpool step and grabbed a pen before he dictated the rest of the words.

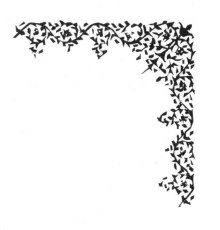

Gold Notebook 1/13/07 3 am
(soul music)

Don't Let Me Lose My Soul

God you put desire in my heart
You gave me feelings and all
You gave me someone to really love
You gave me someone to enthrall

(chorus)

I need you to show me how
Don't let me lose my soul

God you know I want what's right
God I see the end in sight
Though I broke a lifelong vow
Don't let me mess this all up now

God let me do this your way
Please don't take it all away
I need you so much right now
I need you to show me how

(repeat chorus)

God don't let me make mistakes
I will do whatever it takes
Don't let me lose this love
Don't let me lose my soul

(chorus)

I need you to show me how
Don't let me lose my soul

I did some research online and found out that Jaz Bachman was divorced. *Yippee!*

No, wait a minute, I feel guilty about feeling happy that someone was divorced. That is just plain wrong. That has got to be a sin. However, it occurs to me that I am very happy to be divorced. It was quite recently. I don't even want to think about what my marriage was like.

My former friends think nothing of the fact that my former husband is now a divorced Christian. He is still leading what used to be *our* church fellowship group. Neither one of us took drugs or drank. We both fell into the muddy divorce. Yet, for some unknown reason, he came up smelling like a clean fresh rose and I came up smelling like a dirty artificial rose. He never gave any reason for divorcing me and I certainly never figured out why. How come all of our church friends literally stood by him and won't talk to me? Surely there couldn't be a double standard in this day and age? Maybe he is better at public relations than I am. New York is supposed to be a no-fault divorce state but somebody forgot to tell the church.

The minute Rich filed for divorce, I was not invited to the Women's Christmas Tea at church or any other church function. I can see it now: All the women with little scarves tied around their necks, enjoying their little porcelain cups of tea and participating in the cookie exchange. No invitation for me. One woman actually said, "We didn't think you wanted to talk to us."

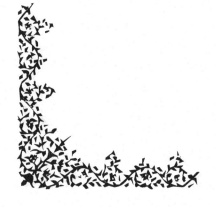

Chapter 2

1/14/07

Dear Pink Notebook,

A message came to me from Jaziel Bachman on Classmates.com, saying that he could send me some demos. Demos? What in the world are demos? Maybe it was a typo and he meant memos. I looked it up in the online dictionary and saw that demos are samples of songs. That's interesting, demos. I wonder whose demos and what kind of demos he's going to send? I hope they're meant to be love songs to me. That's crazy. He probably doesn't really remember me.

1/20/07

Some days have passed and I haven't heard anything from Jaziel Bachman. There are no demos, no messages, nothing. He must think I'm nuts.

No wait a minute, he doesn't know that all I can do is think about him all day long. Funny how high school memories of riding the school bus with Jaz, skipping school, and going to the mall with Jaz seem like memories from last week. I would like to get in an airplane, make a beeline for Jaz Bachman and see if he still has long blond curly hair. He doesn't have any way of knowing that, does he? Unless God tells him that. God wouldn't do that to me, would he? I hope God knows that I wouldn't really run off to Canada. At least, I think I wouldn't.

In case Jaz Bachman ever wants to consider me again, I cannot let him know that I am divorced. I cannot let him know that I am anything less than a perfect person, totally focused on all the right things.

What if he has a girlfriend? What if he has decided he never wants to be in love with anyone again? What if he has a very nice Christian life? What if he wants to be the president, or whatever they call it, of Canada? A relationship with a divorced woman might not be politically correct. I don't know anything about Canada. What would he want with me? I'm a divorced woman. What's worse is that I'm a fake Christian. I put on a show for the whole church acting as if my marriage was perfect. They're right. I'm like an artificial Christmas tree with the branches pointing every which way. The only good place for me is in a box.

1/21/07 3 am

I am sitting alone on the whirlpool step, with my little pink notebook and pen, sobbing silently. Tears are blotting out the words I am writing. I realize that Jaz Bachman is never going to send me any demos, love songs or anything else.

I am deciding that I shouldn't want to rock anybody's boat. I especially don't want to rock Jesus' boat. Anyway, my children would be upset if I involved myself with somebody. They haven't come to accept the fact that their parents have not had a good relationship since who knows when. I had put on a show for them and now they were just beginning to read between the lines of the script.

Forever & Always

Don't send me any demos
I've got your music in my heart

Don't send me any photos
I've had your love from the start

Don't send me any flowers
I remember your scent

Don't send me any promises
That cannot be spent

Just send me a love song
Written from your heart

Just send a tabernacle
With treasures of your heart

Just send me a smile
Wrapped up in a dream

Just send me a future
Made of peaches and cream

I finished writing and hid the notebook under the blue rug in my bedroom.

Blue Notebook

2/3/07 1 pm

Still not getting any messages from Jaz, I have continued to write down what I am hearing in the night and sometimes other times of day, into white for pure, green for refreshing and various other colors and sizes of notebooks.

2/5/07 3 am

Jaz messaged today on Classmates.com that he can't email me, ever. He didn't say why. Maybe he has a girlfriend ... probably somebody who has never been divorced. I couldn't divorce Rich. I didn't think I could support the kids or make the mortgage payments by myself. He theoretically divorced me long before the actual divorce. "Grin and bear it" was my motto. Maybe Jaz is in love with a nice widow. I am putting another soaking wet song in this very blue notebook.

(sounds like blues music)

With a Straw

Somebody sucked my insides out with a straw
All they left was moistened eyes
Don't they know they left me sitting on the wall
With no way down and no compromise

God forgive them now
They don't know what they did today
And I forgive them too
But that doesn't take the hurt away

I feel no malice here for them
Only wish they'd take me back again
Don't know how to enter in
Back into the fold

God are you seeing this
Can you see inside of me
See the space left inside
Where my friend used to be

Be strong be strong now
I tell myself to try
The tears burn on my face
I'm not allowed to cry

This choice is hard now
This sacrifice I make
My life above reproach
The loss for Jesus sake

2/21/07 Green (with envy) Notebook

I told my church fellowship group member, former friend, Joanie Days, that I have been writing a lot of song lyrics. I showed her one lyric called "Photo Radar". She had not spoken to me since my divorce. Of course, she has been married to the same man for forty years. I told her that I started writing once I re-connected online with a friend from high school. She said that I should mail some of the lyrics to him to see what he thinks about them. In other words, she couldn't care less.

Well, since nobody cares, I decided to take her advice and selected thirty-five of the songs that I had written since January 2nd. I typed, printed and sent the lyrics in a manila envelope to Mr. Jaziel Bachman.

12

3/14/07

It's been three weeks, I've heard nothing back from Mr. Jaziel. My supply of Pez is getting very low from continuous nightly trips to the whirlpool desk. Is he taking a long time to read the lyrics? Maybe they are no good. Maybe he thinks I have no business sending him anything. He is probably swamped with important work or lots of girlfriends. Maybe he got the envelope and threw the whole thing in the waste basket or burned it. Maybe Aliens with big heads landed, took the envelope out of the post office and took it to outer space.

3/16/07 Song #109 (Yes, in two and a half months I have written down over a hundred songs.)

I am writing this from what must be Jaz's point of view since there aren't any traffic lights between my lodge, where I live, and my realty office, where I work. I don't speak Spanish but apparently I listen in Spanish.

Monday Morning Loco

Yo' Gringo que' pasa
Are you loco in la cabeza
Andela arriba let's go!
We gotta get to trabajo

Monday morning, I think about you
All day long I think about you
They're all wondering where my head is
Carina, amante novia donde esta tu

Get movin!, you're blockin traffic
Don't you see the light is verde
You got to get it movin Juan
Where is your cabeza man

I'm at work and I think about you
Jugglin thoughts of where to go
And what I have to do
This is like a circus loco!

13

To: AlexaColjen@msn.com
From: JazBachman@msn.com
3/16/2007 00900:00

Hi Alexa,

I wrote some instrumental scores, in January, for a few pieces. I could send you m3ps of Monday Morning Loco, Praise Scraps and Photo Radar.

Jaz

Pink Notebook

3/17/07 Important note to self: The titles "Monday Morning Loco", "Praise Scraps" and "Photo Radar" match titles of lyrics I have written down in notebooks within the last couple of months. I never sent these song titles or lyrics to Jaziel Bachman or anybody or typed these into my Drafts file online. So, he's a composer? Those titles were not in the manila envelope. This is very strange.

I only know poquito Spanish, so I wonder if now he speaks Spanish. Who is supposed to listen to this "Monday Morning Loco"? There is a large Hispanic population in New York but virtually no Hispanics where he lives. This is crazy. Why would he partially title a song in Spanish? When I wrote the lyrics, I didn't even know he was a composer, let alone that he wrote songs with the exact same titles as mine that he didn't know about. My head feels like I am on a Ferris wheel.

To: AlexaColjen@msn.com
From: JazielBachman@msn.com
3/17/2007 001200:04

Hi Alexa,

When I got the songs in the manila envelope, I went nuts.

Jaz

Pink Notebook

3/17/07

Nuts? What does this mean? Is he joking? Is he really nuts and regularly checks into the looney bin? Maybe he didn't respond right away because he was in the looney bin! I don't know what to make of this. Is "nuts" code for something? Maybe I am the one that is nuts.

3/19/07 Song #113 3 am
(rock, the X's are bass drum beats)

Tell Me What I Want

Will somebody tell me
X X X What I want
I'm afraid to say it
I'm afraid to pray it

Somebody tell me
X X X What I want
Put it into words
Read between the lines
Say it's gonna be fine

Tell me how to get there
Tell me it will be fair
Tell me where I'll be
Tell me how to be free

I don't wanna be sorry
Don't want any glory
Just tell me the story
And how it turned out fine

Somebody tell me what I want
I don't wanna say it
I don't wanna pray it
Tell me it turns out fine

3/20/07

Song #116 11 am
I'm reading about Elijah. I do not even like Country Music.
I Kings 17: 1-6 NIV
(country)

Ravens

Lord, sometimes just doin' what's right
I don't know how I'll survive
Fed by ravens in the night
That is how I stay alive

Don't be saddened and depressed
All you need is food and rest
The bread of His broken life
His sparkling water of delight

Hear the gentle whisper say
He only wants you to obey

Fed by ravens in the night
Rest assured God will provide
The bread of His holy life
The flowing water of his delight

Hear the gentle whisper say
He only wants you to obey

Hear the whisper from above
He only wants your love

He only wants your love

Pure White Notebook

3/20/07 3 am I heard part of the harmony, woken from my sleep by its very low tones. I tried to turn off the clock radio, but it wasn't playing. I tried to somehow scribble it on paper. I don't know bass clef. I don't know what I'm doing. I'll try to remember what I heard. It sounded very Catholic and I am not Catholic. However, I do remember that Jaz was raised Catholic.

3/21/07 3 am (I heard the lyrics and am writing them here.)

Holy Altar

Cathedral of the inner life
Where the Holy of Holies lives
Sweet praises rising on a breath
Like a rainbow in the light

Our Holy God
The Trinity
My heart is yours
Live in me

Of the sacrifice from my heart
Of the sacrifice from my heart
Sweet incense rising in a plume
Of the sacrifice from our hearts
Rising praises to the Lord
Our praises fill the room

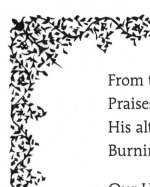

From the altar of sacrifice
Praises rising in one accord
His altar highly carved with grace
Burning praises to our Holy Lord

Our Holy God
The Trinity
My heart is yours
Live in me

3/22/07 3 am

I heard the melody for the "Holy Altar" and played it on my flute, which is now kept in the whirlpool tub. I plunked the melody out on the antique upright piano in the dining hall and tried to write the notes on staff paper. It sounds like the saints singing in heaven.

To: AlexaColjen@msn.com
From: JazBachman@msn.com
3/23/2007 001100:1100

___

Hi Alexa,

I had a vision the other day of some images while waiting in line at McDonald's drive thru. There was a carved wood table with burning incense on it and the smoke was rising in two spiraling columns, joining high in the air. The table was carved with ornate decorations.

Jaz

3/23/07

Dear Pink Notebook,

What am I supposed to make of this? That was certainly not a love note. Is Jaz a Christian? Maybe he became a marijuana smoking, mind blowing, incense burning hippie.

From: AlexaColjen@msn.com
To: JazBachman@msn.com
3/24/2007 0014:3000

_____

Hi Jaziel,

I got a song like that the other day. It's called Holy Altar. There is a harmony and a melody but I don't really know how to write them down. I also do not know how to make chords. I have the words written down.

Alexa

White Notebook

3/24/07 3 am

I heard these words that I know for certain are from God to Jaz.
Song #127 I Kings 19:11 &12 NIV
(marching band with lots of snare)

Stand on the Mountain

Stand on the mountain where you can be seen
Wait for the voice of the Lord
He's not in the hurricane's shattering wind
Or the earthquake of your dream

And when the fire scorches with fear
Don't look for God in there
Do you hear a gentle whisper of faith
That is His voice you hear

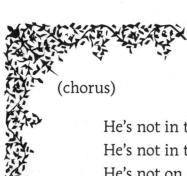

(chorus)

> He's not in the fire
> He's not in the wind
> He's not on a distant shore
> He's right where you stand
> On the mountain top
> In the presence of the Lord

I did not send that anywhere. I typed it onto a Word document at 9 am while looking at I Kings in my Bible, printed it and then put it in a gray folder with an elastic clasp.

Edit Draft Oaks

3/27/07 8 am

As I read my Bible this morning, the words on the page didn't look like what was printed. They looked like song lyrics and I am writing them directly into my e-mail Drafts file.

Isaiah 61 NIV Study Bible
(style: Andrew Lloyd Webber musical)
(alto)

Oaks

> Sovereign God of the universe
> And of my lowly soul
> Who cares about the angels
> And gives what makes me whole
>
> You hear me in the morning
> Rejoicing in your love
> And praising all your goodness
> For caring from above

My adoration for you
For choosing to love me
Is more than I can keep inside
I have to set it free

Your spirit is upon me
Your oil warm and clear
The news of your salvation
From darkness, grief and fear

It's you who gives me beauty
Your smile is on my face
My clothing is your making
Of righteousness and grace

(chorus)

We're like oaks standing tall
Our song flutters in the breeze
God has made us all
Like the strongest of all trees

From: ColjensLodge@yahoo.com
To: JazielBachman@msn.com
3/29/2007 001500:0030

Jaz, thanks for the Happy Birthday emoticons!

I tried to write down a melody on here, I'm not sure if it makes sense.

treble clef starts on middle C
keyboard
style & rhythm: tech pop dance
cut time 1/4=120

CCDEFCDCAA

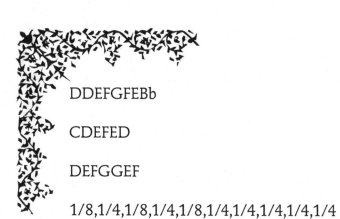

DDEFGFEBb

CDEFED

DEFGGEF

1/8,1/4,1/8,1/4,1/8,1/4,1/4,1/4,1/4,1/4

Spontaneous Combustion

Nobody's ever loved me oh so much
And made me feel oh oh just such
A word a smile a song
Makes me happy all day long!

When you sent me oh oh that smile
It made me sing for oh a while
The song the rose the kiss
It can't get better than this!

I can't contain all of oh this bliss
I just want to shout oh like this
And dance like just I can
Jump up and down bang a pan!

(repeat 1st verse)

Stand on the roof and shout a song
Just wave my arms and run along
And climb up high just for fun
Put on a cape and fly to the sun!

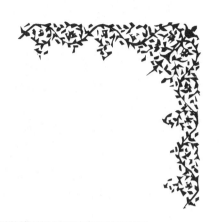

Chapter 3

Colorful Crazy Pattern Notebook

3/30/07 I've driven to Houghton, New York, for the Faith For Music Symposium at the Christian college. I was hoping to learn something about writing lyrics and how to get somebody to write some music to go with my lyrics.

One of the musician/speakers, Sufjan Stevens, said, "Art is a sacred calling in which we participate in all creation. Creativity is a state of innocence and union with the liberty of Christ. Creativity raises us from death to life."

I stayed in a dorm-hotel. In the middle of the night, I wrote down "Head Rush" while looking at a can of Bed Head Hair Spray. Then, inspired by Mr. Stevens, I used the whole can of hairspray to sculpt an extremely creative hair style that stuck out all over my head and went back to bed.

Then, before dawn, I heard lyrics for "Art Baby". I placed my notebook on a little ledge that had a mirror over it. I turned on the light that was over the mirror. I thanked God that I was not sharing the room with anybody.

3/31/07 3 am (I realized that this is the anniversary of Mom's passing and Dad's birthday. I am still amazed that she had a heart attack on his birthday. Then he died a little over a year after that, in July. She always looked half her age and I inherited that attribute.)

(Written at Faith in Music Symposium, while looking at a can of hairspray.)
(God to Me)
(Style: Red Hot Chili Peppers)

Head Rush

A super fine
Super shine spray
Makes you look fine
Makes you shine
That will spread
In your head
When you say
It's my way
That's a head rush
Leads to head mush
Don't let it
Forget it

Just open your eyes
And dream a surprise
Cover your ears and
Listen to what I say
There's grace
For you today
A super fine
Super shine spray
That will cover your head
Go back to bed
Open your eyes
And dream away

That's a head rush
That's a heart gush
That's the super fine
That's the super shine
Spray of grace
When you pray

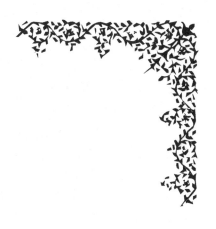

Open your eyes
And dream a sunrise
Cover your ears and
Listen to what I say
There's grace
When you pray
That will cover your head
That's a head rush
That's a heart gush
Go back to bed
Open your eyes
And dream away

That's a head rush
That's a heart gush
That's the super fine
That's the super shine
Spray of grace
When you pray

When I got back to the Lodge, I piled up all the pieces of paper and notebooks and began to transcribe a few of the songs into the Drafts file of my email, starting with "Head Rush". I always dated everything. I put little "notes to self" in parentheses.

Edit Draft Art Baby

3/31/07 5 am
(according to Sufjan Stevens)
(classical, Brahms, lightly, like a lullaby)

Art Baby

Art is a sacred calling
God calling your name
And using your hands to bless Him
And those who live in pain

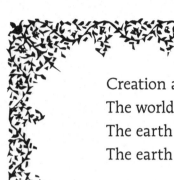

Creation a state of innocence
The world in its infant state
The earth made by His Word
The earth created by the Lord

And when we are creating
A work of innocent art
We find ourselves in union
With God's love and heart

Creation that of God
He made us by His hand
And all that we create
Waits for His command

**Edit Draft This is How I Roll, Homey
4/3/07 6 am**
(rap)

This is How I Roll, Homey

I'm just taking dictation
Transcribing what I hear
Don't give me any credit
For words that just appear

I didn't make up anything
I didn't write one song
I didn't write a melody
It just came along

God wrote all the phrases
All the music, all the lines
He formed every sentence
He made up all the rhymes

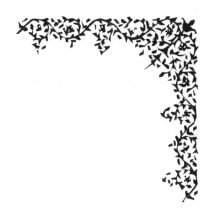

He only used my paper
My computer and my pen
I let Him use all my stuff
Because He's my best friend

Dear Pink Journal Notebook,

I am so tired of being a plastic Christian. On Classmates.com, I messaged Jaz the password to my email, with an invitation to read my Drafts file and see the song lyrics. This way, it is up to him to figure out whether he wants to communicate or not. This is a bold move because there could be rejection involved. I was hesitant but I did it. I put little notes in parentheses for Jaz on the Drafts.

Having the password means that he can also read all my emails. Since I never delete anything, there are 10,476 emails in there. I tried to delete them but it would only let me delete twenty at a time and sixty came in while I was deleting twenty. So I gave up on the entire deleting idea. My life is in that email account. He will know everything there is to know about me and I don't care as long as he sees the Drafts. In fact, not having to pretend anymore is kind of a relief. The ball is in his court.

He will see that I am divorced. He will see that I live in a 13,500 square foot lodge on a private lake. He could praise or condemn me for that. He will see emails like my reply to an email from Sandy. She's someone that I was trying to help with her marriage. I think I would like him to see the good side of me, in case he doesn't remember. One nice thing about an artificial rose is that it doesn't have a bad side. Do I even have a bad side?

Reply From: Alexacoljen@msn.com
To: ssolack@yahoo.com
1/3/2007 001300:0000

Hi Sandy,

You are not a downer! You make me feel like I'm important enough to tell your problems to! At least somebody is talking to me! I spent Christmas all alone.

You need to quit babysitting Darryl! Just go on about your life and let God babysit him! He's not going to find any friends if he stays in the house all the time.

He likes drinking too much beer and watching sports? Why don't you two come over here and he can watch sports while we cook? You can come for supper. I could invite some friendly Christians, if I can find some who are willing to associate with me, now that I'm divorced. You and I will have lasagna and Darryl can eat worms. When do you want to come?

Love,

Alexa

Do You Yahoo!?

Edit Draft Your Song

4/4/07 5:30 am (I am sleeping on one of the couches closer to the home office computer. I literally see colors, purple, gold and green wafting through the air in the home office as the lyrics pour forth. No, I do not, nor did I ever do drugs, smoke weed, not inhale, or anything similar.)

Your Song

The most beautiful thing
I've ever seen
Purple gold and green
And sounding like wine
The fruit of a rhyme
That came from you and me

I hear the strings
The musical things
That make the season bloom
The pictures of trees
With fluttering leaves
That came from you and me

(refrain)

    I hear a brook
    A mountain that shook
    A wind
    A bird
    A tree
    I hear a star
    A beautiful chime
    A song
    A verse
    A rhyme

    Take me to the pasture Lord
    Take me to the blowing grass
    Take me to the sound of love
    Take me where your beat is fast

    Take me where my tears are sweet
    The river's made of wine
    Take me where the power of life
    Lives in color, space and time

(repeat refrain)

4/6/07

Dear Pink Notebook,

Jaz must have used the password to look at my Drafts file. He put music to "Your Song" and sent me an mp3 of it with him singing and playing guitar. I played it over the phone for, Patti, my former sister-in-law. I said that it was a friend of mine singing.

She said, "If that is what he can do with it, you've really got something."

I don't know if she was referring to the lyrics or to the person singing them.

Edit Draft Our Lord

4/7/07 7:30 am (In my home office, as soon as I turned on the computer and opened my poor tattered pink NIV Bible, I saw the printed words as lyrics. I had usually read my Bible in the morning but the words always looked pretty normal before. Nobody could have switched Bibles on me, this one still has the mud stains from when I dropped it in a puddle.)

Jeremiah 23: 6&8 NIV
(good solid beat)

Our Lord of Righteousness

This is the day you are blessed
And I will live in restfulness
In His Name by which we praised
Our Lord of Righteousness

(chorus)

In every place that has a name
That the righteous call their home

As surely as our Lord lives
Who took you to what is home
And from every place that has a name
To what the righteous call their own

All His days you will be saved
And I will live in safety
In His Name by which we praised
Our Lord of Righteousness

And from every place that has a name
To what the righteous call their home

4/6/2007

Dear Pink Notebook,

A real estate broker colleague, Elizabeth Anne Krozychek, invited me to go to the Catholic church with her for Good Friday. She has no idea what is going on with me. I sat in the middle with her. Everyone wears their coat during the service at the Catholic church. I think that is so they can leave faster. I left my coat on, too, but I didn't think about leaving. I sat there crying the whole time. I was crying because I was reminded of the torture and pain that Jesus suffered ... my Jesus. I was crying because he suffered all that for me. Look at me, I am so unworthy. I can't even control my emotions. All I can think about is writing songs and my high school sweetheart. I should be at the Lodge planning another Christian Women's Retreat. What kind of a Christian am I? The very worst kind, obviously.

Edit Draft Veronica

4/6/07 2pm (At St. Dominic's Catholic Shrine, a little splitstone church with stained glass windows and a beautifully carved wood altar with incense burning, on Good Friday)

1/4=88
4/4 time
treble clef, starts on middle G

1/8 pickup note
1/4,1/2,1/8,1/8, barline,1/8,1/4,1/4, musical separation, 1/8, barline,1/4,1/4,1/2 (Hmm, this looks just like us, separated by distance in the same measure but belonging together or could be anyone and God.)

GCDGCDEFEDCD

Psalm 118:109 NIV, and I looked at the Catholic Bible in the book holder on the back of the pew: Sirach 6:14-17

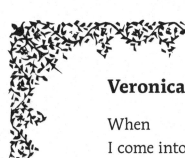

Veronica Wiping the Tears of Her Beloved

When
I come into the sturdy ... house of your love
It's there that I find my very closest friend
When whose pleasant love placed on a perfect scale
Nothing can balance, balance, the other end

(rhythm from first two bars)

When
Drowning in a stream of sorrow
And fearing God and my tomorrows
Not forgetting His first command
It's then that God reveals His plan

(key change)

Though constantly I take my own life
And then give it back to you again
I can't believe the plan for me
So rich and full and true a friend

I can't believe the plan for me
So rich and full and true a friend

What is my role in all of this
What am I supposed to do
Just keep my eyes on the Son of God
And let Him breathe, breathe through you

Just worship Him, the Son of God
And let Him live through you

What is my role in all of this
What am I supposed to do
Just keep my eyes on the Son of God
And let him breathe through you

32

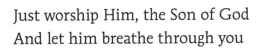

Just worship Him, the Son of God
And let him breathe through you

Just worship Him, the Son of God
And let him breathe through you

What is my role in all of this
What am I supposed to do
Just keep my eyes on the Son of God
And let Him live though you

Just worship Him
Just worship Him
Just worship Him

Edit Draft Transfiguration
4/6/07 1 am
(Matthew 17:2)

Transfiguration

You change me
You make me glow
Brighter than any washing
Brighter than any snow

Your words are rushing through my head
Your smile is fixed before my eyes
I can hear you in my mind
I can feel you in my cries

For your sweet love
For your sweet love

Take me up the mountain
Where your heavenly body glows
Take me where celestial beings
Have their resonance show
Let me take up residence
Where words don't make any sense

Bring me up to your sweet love
To your sweet love
To your sweet love

Alexa,

I would marry you!

Jaz

Dear Fluorescent Hot Pink Journal,

Jaz is definitely reading my Drafts. I wrote Transfiguration about Jesus, but Jaz writes at the end of that Draft that he "would marry" me. Is he serious? He doesn't even know what I look like after thirty-five years. Actually, my looks haven't changed very much. Maybe he would marry me. There are absolutely no pictures of me online. However, I think the interpretation of his remark should be tripled: Spiritually, emotionally, metaphorically.

Edit Draft Why I Hate Airplanes
4/7/07 11 pm

Here's a funny story about how I almost fell out of an airplane with no parachute:

Sometimes, for fun, our family had climbed into one of our airplanes to go for a ride. Maybe we'd go up for about half an hour, circle around, look at the lakes and then land. Sometimes we'd fly to somewhere nearby for lunch. We'd usually take the Aztec because it was a six passenger and that was the size of our family.

On one occasion, we had climbed onto the wing to file into our plane. We were going to fly home from an evening trip. It was a clear, summer twilit evening. Lance, age thirteen, sat in the Co-Pilot seat up front with Captain Rich. Dale and I took the

34

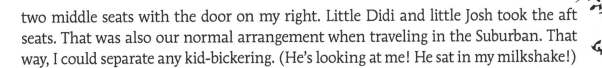

two middle seats with the door on my right. Little Didi and little Josh took the aft seats. That was also our normal arrangement when traveling in the Suburban. That way, I could separate any kid-bickering. (He's looking at me! He sat in my milkshake!)

I took Private Pilot Ground School and I can fly a single or twin engine. I can taxi the plane, read all the gauges, navigate and run the radios. I am a good pilot as long as I don't have to land or take off. I put that in the same category as lawn mowing: Something I know how to do but prefer not to do. This is how I got out of lawn mowing: After protesting without success that lawn mowing is not my cup of tea, I accidentally ran the riding mower into an oak tree.

In the airplane that evening, we only had four sets of headphones with mikes to communicate with each other and the control tower. I let the two younger ones in back have the two sets not being used up front. The children knew not to speak into the microphones once we were in the air. They could listen to their dad and the tower. Everyone belted in. Rich did the pre-check. We taxied into position on runway two-four and I could hear Rich over the engine idle, "Clear."

Then the engine roared and I faintly heard the familiar, "Piper Five Three Zero Four Niner, requesting take off on runway two-four. Over."

They must have rogered because then Rich said, "Thank you. Zero Four Niner. Over".

The plane took off like a knife through soft butter. We made the usual smooth turn and ascended to 3000 feet above sea level at 180 miles per hour. The engine is pretty loud in a twin so nobody was trying to talk. Nobody is supposed to talk through the headset mikes unless it's absolutely necessary. The pilot has to keep the radio clear to hear any towers warning of nearby traffic.

Then, out of boredom, I looked over the control panel. The red light marked "DOOR" was on, indicating that the entry door, right next to me, was ajar. That was pretty common in an Aztec. It looked shut but it wasn't. I unbuckled my seat belt, leaned forward, pulled Lance's headphone off his ear and yelled, "Tell your dad the door is ajar."

Lance put his hand over his mike and yelled to his dad, "The door's not shut!" That was pretty smart of him not to put that information through the headset, that way the tower didn't pick it up. Taking off with the door not shut has got to be some kind of a violation.

Rich glanced back at the door, and in one instant, reached back past me and unlatched the door, while at the same time whipping the plane into a sharp left turn! My seat belt was still off! I screamed my head off, grabbed the door handle with both hands and tried to pull it shut. The power of the wind was tremendous. My long hair and loose blouse were being sucked out the two inch opening! I couldn't pull it shut! I screamed, "Dale! Help me shut the door!"

Dale, age sixteen, calmly unbuckled his seatbelt, leaned over me, grabbed the handle over my two hands and pulled. Dale is really strong. The handle pulled right off the door. I screamed even louder. I grabbed onto the seat in front of me with one hand and with the other I grabbed the vinyl covering and stuffing on the inside of the door where the handle used to be. Dale hung onto my shoulders and pulled. My hair and blouse were still blowing out the gap. This really concerned me because if I was going to plummet and be found dead in someone's front yard, I wanted to be fully dressed.

I looked at Pilot and Son in the front seats. They were calmly face forward, chewing gum. They couldn't hear anything with their headsets on.

I started screaming, "Dale! Tell Dad to land!"

Now the vinyl was ripping off the door. Dale had been previously sternly instructed never to distract Dad when Dad is flying. Instead, he decided to lean forward, knock Lance's headphone aside, and calmly tell Lance to land the airplane. Lance doesn't know how to land or fly, he just listens to the tower in the headphones.

Lance, not realizing the severity of the situation behind him, started laughing. Dale always said he wanted to land the minute we took off to fly anywhere.

Just then, Rich glanced back to see why Dale was leaning forward without a seat belt.

"Land it!" I screamed.

Maybe he didn't read my lips correctly because Captain Rich just kept flying for what seemed like a very long time. After all, he's the Captain, not me. I figured he was weighing the alternatives ... wife falling out of airplane or request emergency landing. Both options could mean a violation with a penalty for him for not noticing the red "DOOR" light prior to takeoff. I saw his mouth move as he said something to the tower.

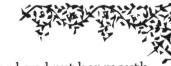

Little Didi took her headphones and seatbelt off, leaned forward and put her mouth up to my ear, "Dad said we have squirrels in the airplane and we're landing."

Little Josh just kept calmly looking out the window, like he did since the day he was born. He talked when necessary.

Rich made a nice landing. As we taxied to park, the uniformed young man waved us in with red flashlights, caught my eye, smiled and did an eye-roll.

When we all got out of the plane, I asked Rich, "Squirrels?"

He looked at me like it was all my fault, "I didn't want a violation, so I told them it was getting a little squirrely up there."

"I suppose that's one way of putting it," I said very sweetly.

He had thought that the wind would shut the door if he completely freed the door from its latch while making that sharp turn. Unfortunately, Rich never took any physics classes. I ran to the very necessary plumbing facilities in the little FBO office. I ran back to the plane and made sure my shirt was sufficiently tucked in. Then we all got back in the plane, pulled the door shut, checked that the red light wasn't on and flew back to our nice safe Lodge.

Edit Draft Risk My Life
4/8/07 3 am (This song is green and gold, I can see its colors, do you hear the music for this?)

Risk My Life

(me)

> I'm like a fluttering leaf
> Falling from a tree
> Catch me before I hit the ground
> Don't let the wind blow me around

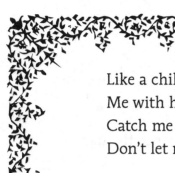

Like a child on a slide
Me with happiness inside
Catch me before I hit the ground
Don't let me go falling down

(you)

I am here to hold you up
Here to fashion you the cup
To give your thirsty lips a drink
To hold your hand while you think

To give you water from a spring
To give you sunshine and a ring
To love you more than life on earth
To love you with all that I am worth

(chorus)

Risk my life
Have it all
Take my love
Don't let me fall

Risk My Life comment by Jaz:

4/8/07

Alexa,

THIS one, RISK, grabbed me right away. I'm jammin it up with my students. Soft synth pad with guitar, long melismatic melody, preternaturally beautiful chords fluttering in a tropical night breeze. I need to take a month off to write all of these songs, I'm going to bust.

Jaz

Dear Pink Notebook,

Jaz must still be reading my Drafts file because he actually made a comment after reading my Draft of "Risk My Life". He wrote right at the bottom and saved the whole thing as a new Draft. It's amazing what someone will do if they just have your password.

Edit Draft God With Us

4/9/07 5 am (I know you have this music in you, I hear you playing it on guitar.)
(I see red and orange, oh I get it: Fire!)
(driving beat)
(1/8, 1/8, dotted half, 1/4, dotted half)

God With Us

I will praise you Lord
(echo) I will praise you Lord

(1/8, 1/8, 1/8, 1/4, 1/4, 1/8, 1/8, 1/8)

For every thought and every line
For your goodness all the time
I will praise the name I love
Emmanuel is God With Us

I will fill my cup

(echo) I will fill my cup

With your Holy love

(echo) With your Holy love

I will feast till the evening dies
I will drink till the earth goes dry

I will praise you Lord

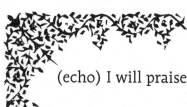

(echo) I will praise you Lord

I will hear your love for me
I will sing for I am free
I will praise the name I love
I will love the God with us

I will praise the name I love
Emanuel is God with us.

(Jaz, I have put a lot more songs into a secret Pink Notebook. They are secret. Funny how that word "secret" sounds a lot like "sacred.")

Edit Draft American Stamp

4/9/07 8:30 am (just flowing with no mistakes and no changes and I hear you, Jaz, singing it)

(I see a single cloud in the sky and it looks like an eagle on a postage stamp.)

Isaiah 40:31 NIV

American Stamp

He will carry you with eagles wings
Though we don't understand these things
He'll lift you in their mighty claws
And bring you to a place of love

And then we'll soar to the mountain top
We'll fly in his care
We'll love like a morning dove
Who's always been there

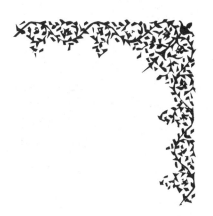

And I'll climb the steepest hill
And cling to the rock
I'll find my sure footing
As I hear my Lord talk

Grieve for your heartache
Beleaguer your sin
Know that His Spirit
Is destined within

Love without ceasing
Dream without cause
Believe for the future
In the power of God

(PS I don't know what beleaguer means and I don't have time to look it up.)

Pink Notebook

4/10/07 I am sitting in the telescope observatory room of the Lodge, in the afternoon sunlight from the three story window on the lake side. I'm sitting on a little bench. I have a little square scrap of paper on which I wrote in February and a pen. The paper has lyrics written in pencil. The Lodge is empty. All 13,500 square feet of it are silent. I'm sitting here crying silently. That's probably a habit learned from not being allowed to cry out loud. The scrap has teardrops on it and the drops are washing off the words. As I begin to write with the pen, I hear the melody for the lyrics on the scrap as I transfer the words neatly to you, Secret Pink Notebook. I am not typing them into my Drafts file.

(God's way: Me to God)

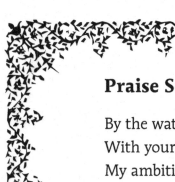

Praise Scraps/By the Water

By the water when I wait
With your love you heal me
My ambition growing faint
From my, From my, From me

By the water when I wait
Of my sin you heal me
By the water when I wait
Peace within you give me

Leave me--don't ever
Go away--don't ever
Without you I can't live
My joy, my peace you give

Forever I'll love you
With you I must stay
By the water I can't wait
For even one more day

4/11/07

Dear Pink,

I had found out before (but after I wrote the pencil lyrics) that Jaz already composed an instrumental piece called Praise Scraps. When he finally did email his instrumental demo to me, this morning, the music matched my lyrics, exactly. He has never seen my lyrics.

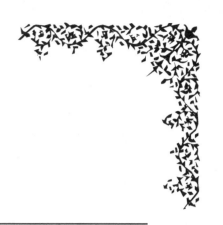

Chapter 4

Edit Draft Kurt Vonnegut

4/12/07 9 pm

(From AP online news article: "Kurt Vonnegut Dies", I am reading the obituary online but the lines of words look all wavy to me. I see it as lyrics and am writing them onto the screen.)

(I had read one of Vonnegut's books when I was clinically depressed during the year I had the blood disease and ended up in the hospital. I was nineteen at the time. I don't remember much of what it said. I do remember that it said that wine is a good cure for depression.)

Ecclesiastes NIV: Everything is meaningless.

Kurt Vonnegut

You really didn't save us
But you threw out a line
Your book was like a life raft
A square of white in a sea of lime

When darkness and fear overcame us
You related to the place
Where nothing really mattered
No smile was on our face

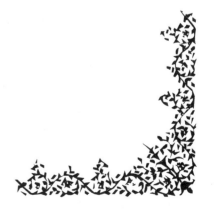

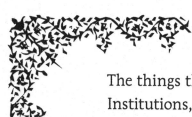

The things that man created
Institutions, Cats and War
Don't make any sense at all
Less than an empty ocean floor

You didn't have the answers
You didn't think you knew
But you didn't think they all did
You were a seeker of the truth

You mostly played the front row
With Cats and Slaughterhouse Five
What was War really about
Aren't we fighting to stay alive

What is war really about
Aren't we killing to stay alive

What is war really about
Are we dying to stay alive

Edit Draft Prisms of Clouds

4/12/07 1 am (I was awakened with an actual vision in my bedroom of man-sized, six foot prisms reflecting clouds and I heard these lyrics.)

Prisms of Clouds

Lonely prisms made of glass
Encasing clouds of glory
Father beckons from the past
Telling me the story

Chandelier of heavens light
Reflecting when my eyes close
Where is all that is in sight
Only when my heart knows

(chorus)

> A moving space in time
> A legend rich with rhyme
> A generation's wine
> A world that's only mine
>
> Where are your songs
> Where are your chimes
> Where are the verses
> That make up the signs

(bridge)

> Where are the promises
> Where are the chords
> Where are the sepulchers
> That honor His word

(melody key change)

> Clearly prisms made of glass
> Large as life with reputation
> Holding clouds of Water's love
> Full of loving affirmation
>
> Then a rushing wind
> That twinkles every chime
> Rises from within
> And brings the world to time
>
> The symphony begins
> The sound a melody
> My heart contains the words
> And loves the final Three

Edit Draft Primrose Day

4/19/07 2 pm (While I was looking at a little story in a magazine about a poor blind girl named Allison, I saw the story as song lyrics. Thank you, God, for this flower of a song and its sweet perfume. It smells so good because it is from you.)

Primrose Day (today)

After walking through the garden
I went to Lexa's place
I imagined the cute little girl
Who couldn't see my face

Reclining in the light of God
Hearing songs she heard from me
Lace was in front of her
Money clinking 'round the tree

She never stopped her humming
Even when she heard that sound
Her face was sweet and calm
Not bothered by the world around

I kneeled to place a flower
On the apron of her fears
I could see her excitement
As she sensed the flower there

A million scented memories
A miracle about to unfold
Her face brightened into joy
As she heard the story told

She laid her music down
Reaching for the fragrance
The fragrance of pure grace
She grasped it with her hands

She held it to her heart
That was the very best part

Edit Draft NASA

4/19/07 9 pm

(Right now, I am looking online at images of galaxies and also an image of the earth taken from space at night with cities lit. I see and hear lyrics. My heart is beating very fast, my face is pink.)
(an apocalyptic prophetic vision)
(dissonant music background over spoken word)

NASA

First screen, God's two eyes
Watching the earth
Second screen, God closes his eye
On the little birds

Gibraltar Straits a key
Europe is in the dark
Lost in their sins
Oppressed from within

The mountain stars
Are where we are
Where we are free
Swiss Alps hold the Majesty
The whiteness of snow
Where the Holy go

Iceland looks like a caribou
Its horns like angel wings to you
Black sea a rising smiling Bear
Red sea they come from everywhere
Back to Israel

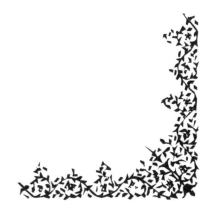

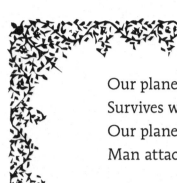

Our planet the Indian warrior
Survives without something to take
Our planet is at the bottom
Man attacked by the snake

The fall of man over Africa
America follows the story
Australia an innocent bunny
What an allegory

America remains in her sin
The shadow of Canada
Almost within
Leftists kicked in the shin

Spectacular!
A never before seen explosion!
Light darkness and erosion!
Destruction Blood and Corrosion

Islas de la Madera
Where we will dive
Spain, France and England
They will survive

Africa and Italy
Are total losses
The birds survive
And Green Island crosses

Grande Sao Paulo, Rio de Janeiro
Salvador (dies)
A beautiful horizon separates
The Brazilian Platform in northern skies

The Florida coast
Recife, Fortaleza
Die in their pleasures
Where nobody sees ya
Inland they just survive
Brasilia, Georgia,
Some in the upper lands die
We tried, we really tried

Northwestern America
And the same in Canada
Alaska stays in the picture
Mexico is a disaster

The biggest explosions
are the cities of lights
New York, Washington
Philadelphia, Chicago
Miami, Houston, Dallas, Detroit
The Yucatan Peninsula is gone
Northern California remains strong.

It isn't magic
But our children need to know
They have to be warned
So they know where to go

Edit Draft Heart Pain

4/21/07 (I got kicked in the thigh at karate class and there was a big bruise and aneurism. Then my heart started hurting while I was in the kitchen baking a strawberry pie. I called my daughter, Didi, who told me to go to the emergency room. I waited a few hours to see if I'd feel normal and then drove myself to the hospital after I realized that I hadn't felt normal since the recurrence of Jaz and maybe was never to be henceforth. Besides, first I wanted to have a piece of strawberry pie.)

(Written in the emergency room 4/20/07 11pm till 4/21/07 10am, I heard lyrics the whole time and wrote them into a little notebook that I had brought in my purse.)

John 14:1, 27 NIV "Let not your heart be troubled. Trust in God ... and do not be afraid."

(operetta in a high soprano)

Heart Pain

I've never been so afraid
Not of dying
But of not ever seeing you
Before I do

I must have been in a crash
I'm hooked to every chord
I'm crying out of breath
I'm calling for my Lord

My heart is in such pain
I ache for you inside
I cannot tell the nurse
Where the diagnosis lies

Please give me one last moment
To only hear your voice
Please give me one more chance
To make the bravest choice

And if I die tonight
Then who will let you know
Who will answer your question
Or tell you where to go

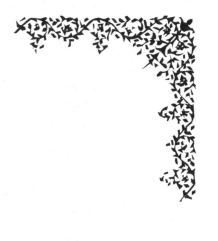

You would be unknowing
And missing my funeral hug
Not knowing some of our songs
Are in books kept under rugs

I'm thinking of you writing
The songs I left behind
The only way to love me
Part of me that survived

Dumped me onto a stone cold slab
See through me
Motion stilled
An X is what they see

I H S
It's three
They want to hear a sound
God finds me

I'm under a rock
Where there is no ground
Help from the angels
They're here all around

We'll wait here till morning
To hear music sound
We'll wait here till morning
To hear music sound

They'll find us with "Radar"
They'll look under Blues
They'll search the computer
For underground tunes

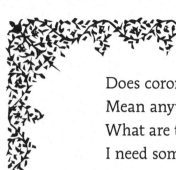

Does coronary thrombosis
Mean anything to you
What are they saying
I need some new shoes?

Her legs will not take her
Where she wants to go
Only in the Spirit
Can her song birdies go

I need your assurance
That my life's not a loss
And that only in Jesus
By way of the cross

How can I wonder
When I am so sure
You are the answer
You are the cure

I feel like an oyster
Waiting for a pearl
How much more chafing
I am "Just A Girl"

How much heparin
Applied to the lock
How much more bruising
Against the hard dock

Set my vessel free now
Set my sails to the wind
Set my heart to the sunrise
Take the hurt from my shin

And here now and now hear
My lesson of love
It's clear as a bell tone
Like the song of a dove

"Though you look like a train wreck
There's nothing wrong with you."
"Thy Word is hid in my heart
That I might not sin against you"

I can't take it all in
Too much to see and do
I don't want to be anywhere
That doesn't include you

(8:30 am)

That's your cue
Every six, four, two
Couplets of a rhyme
God hears us every time

For a while I thought for sure
Lexicon picture was last you'd see
I thought for sure in a blur
My death was meant to be

It looks like dawn has risen
The pictures clear and true
It's only going to be a time
Till I am there with you

No, the flow was blocked
I'm totally shocked
The result had come in slow
Help me God! I don't want to go

Set me with the gel
On my nice lean thighs
Touch my pressure points
Squeeze me I'm alive

Sylvan river runs with zest
Quicksilver through my veins
Fireworks blew white and red
The Venus machine runs like a train

Jubilation! Fire and heat!
Shouts to God! Amen!
Life is glorious! Life is sweet!
I'm going to live again!

The techie sang before I dressed
Because I passed every test
Sitting in clean white blankets
Then I really got blessed

You look like a dolly
That made a big nest
Thank God and everyone
The Great Doctor is the best!

Edit Draft Death is Funny

4/22/07 3 am

(God must think my emergency room, partially psychosomatic, partially factual symptoms of a couple nights ago warrant waking me up in the middle of the night for a laugh.)

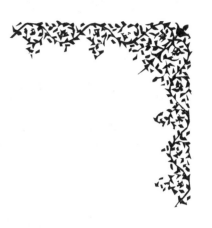

Death is Funny

Somebody kicked my shin
And from the clot I'm gonna die
Gotta go to emergency
Wait, just a bite of pie

Hello reception lady
Don't make me stand in line
Tell them there's no pulse
That will make them fly

Hook her up to everything
Put oxygen in her nose
Lay her down for x-ray
That's not a sexy pose

She doesn't trust the doctor
Not sure about the nurse
What is that she's writing
In the notebook from her purse?

Everything looks OK
We have the insurance card
Let's run every test we've got
That shouldn't be too hard

This could take a while
She doesn't seem to care
Throw some blankets on her
She can sleep right there

The same thing happened to her
When she didn't want to go
To kindergarten round up
Well, whoever could have known

Blue Notebook

4/26/07 6am (It's a gray day today at the Lodge. It's too foggy to see the water. Yes, that's right. That means what you think it means.)
(a bluesy, floosy thing)

Fish Food

There's no sunrise here
It's pouring rain
Cloudy, gray and
Full of shame

A darkened pool
Catches the drops
Surrounded by
A bastion of rocks

It's cold and damp
Dark and dreary
Full of sounds
Oh so eerie

Inside the lodge was full of life
Children drank the spring
Strength walked upon the wood
Heard the songbirds sing

Power and light
Linens and glass
Fire and songs
All moved so fast

The rain has stopped
Light is a wish
After a rain
There's food for the fish

Edit Draft In Eternity

4/30/07 6 am (This was spoken out loud, by me, at 6 am in my sleep. It woke me up. I heard myself saying the words and I saw the colors and shapes.)

In Eternity

"Yellow triangle
Purple triangle"
Our passion and our fear

Silver sunset
Golden sunrise
Our birth and our years

Pileated woodpecker
Flaming red head
Our sins and our desires

Winchester engraving
Calendars and events
Our fate and our timers

Holy God
Can you see
Our lives are destined
In eternity

Holy God
Can you see
Our lives are destined
In eternity

4/29/07 I had written the following explanation for the <u>Listen to Your Momma</u> Writing Contest, which I won. My lyrics for "Susan" were recently published in both paperback and e-book versions.

"One time, when I was in high school, five of my good friends were going to go on a winter weekend camping/skiing trip. My boyfriend, Jaz, and I had both wanted to go. I really wanted to go with them, but my mother said I couldn't. She didn't have any reason. I begged her and cried. She said no, so it was no. I was really mad at her. I went to my room and slammed the door.

On Monday morning at school, the English teacher announced that all five of the students that had gone on the trip had died. The road was icy and Susan, who was driving, was speeding and had passed a car on a curve. I couldn't hear the rest of the story, I was so shocked. I saw that the teacher's lips were moving but I didn't hear anything else. I would have been in that car. Jaz would have been in that car.

All of the kids were smart, conscientious kids. Susan's father was a doctor. There was not one thing anybody could do about it now.

Now I think, why did this happen to such a nice family? Why didn't God do something? My Pastor said that when bad things happen we have to remember that God did do something. God did do something when he sent Jesus.

Sometime after the funeral, when some of us went to Susan's house, we saw that her mother had made a little shrine on one of the tables. There were pictures of Susan and some things she had won. There was a big empty place where Susan had lived in the hearts of the people that loved her."

Susan

Susan, you were our friend
We loved you till the end.
We didn't know what you'd do
We didn't know or have a clue

We missed you back at school
We all thought you were so cool
We loved your pretty hair
Your smile and ways so fair

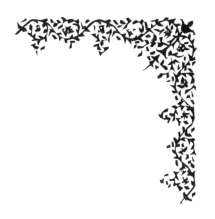

My mother said I couldn't go
How on earth did she know?
That would have been my last day
God would have taken me away

We don't know why He took you
Why he took the others too
We can only hope and pray
We'll see you again some day

Now I tell my children
Don't do what Susan did
Remember Susan is what I say
That is what I say and pray.

4/23/07 I have been sleeping on one of the couches closer to the home office computer. Spoons was written directly onto the computer screen. Apparently God doesn't really need paper or pens. He might need only a Word document window.

(jazzy)

Spoons

(me to Jesus)

Thanks for praying for me
He's turning me every which way from sin
I should buy a lottery ticket
I would probably win

God says He misses me
Doesn't want me out of line
He says He has some promises for me?
They're the very best kind

Here I am I'm listening Lord
I'm where I'm supposed to be
You know it's not unusual for a girl like me?
I'm always up at three

Except for last night Lord,
Dude, what was up with that?
I slept through the whole long night Lord?
You knew where I was at

I let you sleep, Babe
Sometimes I know you need some rest?
My promises are still here
I always save the best

This is a cool looking song Lord
And I can hear the tune
I like how all the verses
Look like little spoons

Except that one, Babe
Don't think you always know so awfully much
I just want to show you
I always keep in touch

Is that the promise, Lord?
That you'll always be just right there?
You'll always be with me
To show me that you care

That's the promise, Babe
I'm here to write and sing your tunes
Be careful how you write them down
Watch your little spoons

Edit Draft Ray

4/23/07 5 am to 6:30 am

(Written directly onto the screen while reading an online news article: India Celebrates Rai-Bachchan Wedding, dated April 20, 2:22 pm ET. Interpretation: Spiritually, world prophetically, people around us)

(It's 5 am! Let's get up and dance!)

(definitely India sound,1/4 tones? India Dance rhythm)

Ray of Sunshine

Mumble jumble India humbled
Jaded eyes of the world
Ray of sun and turbaned king
Celebrate their great wedding

The wedding of the century
Melodrama of Hollywood
Secrecy, dance, romance
This has got to be good

(chorus)

Masala Bung Rah!
It's your wedding day!
Come here! Come here!
Keep away! Keep away!

Bacchus with his gold and crème
Your face veiled with flowers
On a white stallion riding
Dancers round for hours

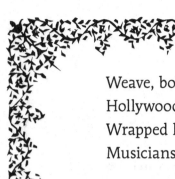

Weave, bob and punch the air
Hollywood covered with blood
Wrapped his head in sinful thoughts
Musicians bringing the crud

Then into the refreshing tent
Spacious and fragrance filled
Gold curtains surround the garden
Trumpets, drums and symbols (cymbals)

(repeat chorus)

Garlands and wedding vows
Inside the barricades fold
Was she wrapped in sin?
Or with lovely cream and gold

Two years apart in their age
In January
They were engaged
Pictured in the public eye

Sunshine had the attention
In nineteen ninety-four
Worldly determination
Recognized her on the floor

(repeat chorus)

Starring with recognition
Commercials overseas
Cosmetic representative
And cola companies

Back then he was famous
His father a great lege'
His mother famous for acting
She's a lot like J

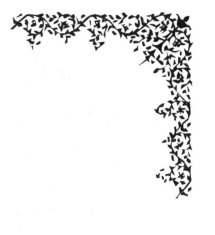

The road was paved with breezes
Trees and buildings scaled
Others peered around them
Their ambitions failed

(repeat chorus)

Bitter mumble jumble
Outside the creamy home
The poor jealous woman
Had nowhere to roam

She had a promise of marriage
A dancer in a music video
She thought she was a ten
When he starred two years ago

He doesn't even talk to her
She really wants to know
They take her to the hospital
Then off to jail she goes

Finally released
In twenty thirty eight
Authority is on to her
Media thinks it's great

(repeat chorus)

Edit Draft Don't

4/25/07 3 am (I was peacefully sleeping with a blanket on one of the couches closer to the home office. God woke me up with this conversation between Himself and me.)

Don't Say

Don't say swear words.
Don't say swear words?
That's why you woke me up at three?
Yes, don't say swear words,
Take those out of your vocabulary.
Huh?
You heard me.
And stop thinking about how some good words
Sound like some bad words.
God, I can't get away with anything.
That's the general idea.

It's not my fault,
I was married to a construction worker.
Every other word would offend.
Don't blame it on the Captain,
No more need to pretend.

You weren't raised with that,
That's not what you were taught,
Just be the way I made you,
Don't repeat what he had brought.

OK, I got it Lord,
Don't remember and don't repeat,
Whatever he brought,
Isn't my beef.
Right.

Whatever he did
Whatever he said,
If it's not my condition,
Then just eat some Pez.
(silence/rest)
Well, Lord that rhymes.
Then just go to bed.

Edit Draft Barking Dogs

4/25/07 (From online AP news article: "Democrats Predict they can win Iraq vote. I read the story online, this evening, but see it in rhyming stanzas. I don't have to think about it, it just flows out. Maybe it's a rap song. Triple interpretation: literally, spiritually, personally)

Barking Dogs

Predictions of the house
Saying what will pass
The President will veto
US troops to leave Iraq

Members of the house
Going along with the party
Despite their desire
For early withdrawing

Wednesday's child
General Petraeus
House scheduled voting
Impending chaos

A showdown with Democrats
Over Bush's faith promise
Emboldened by election
Which handed them Congress

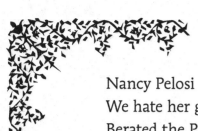

Nancy Pelosi
We hate her guts
Berated the President
In her voting records

The hundred billions bill
Sets a nonbinding goal
Of completing the pullout
By the first of April

Troops could remain
After two thousand eight

For noncombat missions
Counterterrorism of late

The bill to negotiate
Will reach the desk
After Senate vote Thursday
The week is next

Democrats view November
And their total control
As a referendum on conduct
Bush's running the war

Bush is firm on his strategy
For winning the war
Counterproductive
The call for withdrawal

"Commanders in combat zone
Would take fight plans at will
Six thousand miles by phone
From lawmakers on the Hill"

"The enemy's advantage
And a danger for our troops"

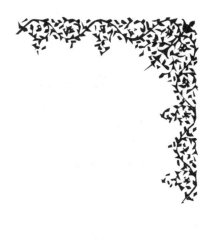

Whether Democrat leaders
Had it in them to remember
Originally demanding ending
On a line of September

Several of the members
Agreed to back Emanuel
Even though they wanted
Troops to be with Samuel

Democrats will
Send the bill
Hoping for a change of heart
But they don't expect it

We are very hopeful
The president will sign
Will change his mind
And set new policy for engagement

Democrats with slim margins
In both houses two ways
Are unlikely to override
With insults traded Tuesday

Blind opposition
To strategy in the war
Chains accusing reeds
Of vying for more seats

Cynically believing
That all is lost
Political advantage
Barking dogs.

Edit Draft Dry Ice

4/26/07 11:50 pm (These lyrics are a combination of a dream from 3 nights ago, and a newspaper article: *Daily Telegram*, Wed Apr 25, "PLANET DISCOVERED Big step taken in search for "life in the universe".)
(coldly emotional)

Dry Ice

Waiting on the balcony
In someone else's gown
Looking at the young man
Looking at his crown

Rushing in the morning
With a backpack full of cares
You wear a blue spring jacket
As you are downstairs

(chorus)

Life in the universe
Is it here or is it far
Life in the universe
It's here if you are

No time for warm pancakes
Only dry ice in a cup
That's what you wanted
That's what will fill you up

(bridge up)

A cup of cold water
In the name of the Lord
Only cold water
Is what we can afford

(repeat chorus)

> You're heading downtown
> Where we went to school
> I'll buy ice for tomorrow
> That's the new rule

(repeat chorus)

Hi Pink!

4/27/07 5 am

It is during the drought of no communication from Jaz in weeks, A-hah! The light just went on! "Dry Ice"! It takes me a while sometimes. When this one melts, i.e., when it's no longer in chunks of words and chunks of music but melted together into words with music, when Jaz and I collaborate, we're going to mix my words, his music and have a life! We're gonna have soda water! Melted dry ice is soda water! We're gonna have a life-filled, happy party praising God! Water equals Spirit! This is all very scientific.

Edit Draft Time to Mesh

5/3/07 5am
(Time to mesh! From God to us!)
(It's a round)
(calliope sound, like a merry go round)

Time to Mesh

It's time to mesh the gears!
Start up the music machine!
Time to tell the story
Of John 3:16!

Get up! Get up!
How can anybody sleep!
It's time to tell everyone
Time to feed the sheep!

(This chorus is resurrected out of Pink Notebook, 1/28/07 3am, "Walking Next to You"!)

Love never forgets
Love never can hide
Love never retreats
Love's a feeling inside

(back to melody)

This is too exciting
Don't waste another day
Get on the horse and ride
Don't let it slip away!

All those little choruses
Dig them up and mesh
Put it all together
I will do the rest

Put yourself aside
Put aside your pride
You can do this now
I will show you how

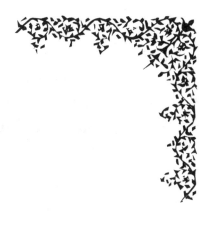

(repeat chorus)

> I love both of you
> Everyone around you too
> I see your willing heart
> I've seen it from the start
>
> Be strong and listen close
> Try to make the most
> Of every single day
> Don't let it slip away

Edit Draft Compressed

5/4/07 (midnight: 30)
(slow and sweet with violins)

Compressed

> If every love song ever written
> Was rock and rolled into one
> It couldn't be half as free
> As the one about you and me
>
> And if every love story written
> Was made into one long book
> It wouldn't be half as good
> As even just one look
>
> And if all of those great writers
> Like Dylan, Shakespeare and Keats
> Made just one long sonnet
> It wouldn't be any great feat

Our love starts on the point of a star
And travels to Venus, Jupiter and Mars
Our love starts on the mountain snows
And dives ocean depths where no man goes

Our love is endless like God before time
And our love is boundless like air in the sky
And our love is hotter than the center of suns
And massive like fusion in the center of atoms

Everybody means well
But they don't have a clue
They can't see inside us
They don't know what to do

They don't have the answers
But we know it's God's way
We'll just take each day
As long as God lets us pray

Edit Draft Wildfire Scare

5/12/07 8:30 am (While looking at an AP online news article, dated one hour eleven minutes ago: "Calif. Island Survives Wildfire Scare". I saw the words as lyrics. Don't ask me, I just write 'em, but this is obviously about gay men getting their ideas from bad music; God's judgment on homosexuality; and the chorus is about how young people need to hear good stuff when they're in their cars.)

(verses: raucous, blaring)
(chorus: innocent, soft)

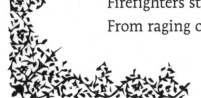

Wildfire Scare

Catalina Island struggling
With normal pictures, hosts   (they were making a travel brochure)
Firefighters stopping wildfire
From raging off the coast

Normal tourists take tours
Ferries tour the beach   (fairies)
Hitting their white balls
And lounging in the reach

A melted ball of plastic   (just one burnt golf ball was left)
The ground a charred black hole
Stay away from Catalina
Thirty-five feet from your door

Broadcasting Satan's music
Sparking men's interior station   (radio station burned)
One home is pinpointed (only one house, owned by gays, burned)
As the example for the nation

(chorus)

America's eaglets   (baby eagles weren't harmed)
Untouched by human hands   (innocent children)
Pure, unadulterated
Milestones in our land   (as the next generation goes, so goes the nation)

5/13/07

Dear Pink,

Still at the Lodge, still writing in the middle of the night. Jaziel Bachman is still 2000 miles away. From day one in January, I have had him on my mind. He must think that all these are generic songs. Just like white cans of corn on the shelf, they could be made by anybody for anybody. I guess some of them are a little corny.

5/13/07 6 am (Sleep? What's that?)
(Definitely a twangy country song)

Holy Ghost Rider

I'll take out today's paper
And bring in today's trash
What have I been thinkin'?
I just have to crash

(Chorus)

Holy Ghost Rider (writer)
Ridin down the line (Writin')
Pony Express delivery
Slow but sure on time

Bring me up some ketchup
I need it for my cake
And some chocolate ice cream
For the hot dogs I'm gonna make

Chapter 5

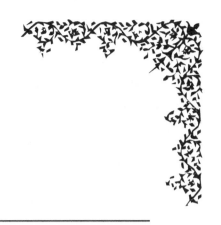

5/15/07 1 am to 3 am with a little crying jag in the middle

Dear Pink Private Notebook,

It's 1 am. I can't leave the Lodge. I have my work here. Maybe Jaz can move here. My grown kids live in this state. I would miss them. I have no extra money. Am I even supposed to go to Canada? My thoughts are not pure and holy! I'm sure I can think of some more excuses not to go. A very wise Reverend, David Thompson, once said to me, "If you're looking for an excuse, any excuse will do." I am going to use the excuse that I can't find my hiking boots. How about that I can't find the cords (chords)?

Red Chords

Lord you're law is impossible to keep
Is this some kind of a test?
Are you just tired of seeing me weep?
I'm sure a failure of the rest

I can obey on the outside
But inside I'm as guilty as sin
I made the first bad move
Lord, I'm sorry I just can't win

Now there's no turning back
I've tried everything I know
No way for me to get on track
I know where this has to go

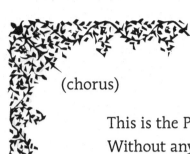

(chorus)

This is the Pastor's sermon
Without any notes
That's what you're telling me
Without any quotes

It's all about obedience
About doing what I'm told
Even when I don't feel like it
Even till I get real old

It's about trusting you
Like that song "Trust and Obey"
"To be happy in Jesus
Cause there's no other way"

I have to be an example Lord
How I suffered just for your cause
So children can look up to me
When they want to break laws

So they can hold the fort down
So they can grab your hand
So they will brave the gale force
Threatening to take their man

My suffering isn't so great Lord
Look at the soldiers' past
Look at what they remember
Their friends burned in a blast

Look what they have to carry
Look what they cannot shake
Look how there's no forgetting
There's no hard choice to make

All so I could have freedom
The same as you did Lord
You suffered for my freedom
The symbol of the red cord

(I'm crying too much I can't write any more now.)

OK I'm doing the trust thing
I see you've been doing your part
I see all the little ways
You answered prayers of my heart

I'm going to keep on trusting
I see things falling in line
I'm going to be brave and steadfast
Your timing is always fine

You have what's best for me
As long as I choose to obey

You always have the answers
As long as I go your way

If it wasn't for you I'd be dead
Lord, I just love you too much
No way will I ever disobey
Land in hell with the Devil's touch

No way would I ever leave you
There's danger in what I just said
Peter who said he'd never deny
John who just obeyed till he died

(repeat chorus whenever)

Edit Draft Reward

5/19/07 1 am (I plunked some of this out on my keyboard, Friday night. John 10: 27, 35, 38, 42 NIV)
(this is rockin', modern rock beat, 1/4=120)

Reward

What I tell you in the night
Speak in the white daylight

I will turn a daughter
Against her mother
A daughter-in-law
Her mother-in-law

(chorus)

1/4 1/4 1/4 1/8 1/2dot
E E E D E
    What man finds his life

1/8 1/8 1/4 1/4 1/4 1/8 1/2dot
D D E E E D B
    Will be losin' what he finds

E E E D E
    What man loses his life

D E E E D E
    Will find His peace of mind

A A A G A
    In the name of the Lord

G A A A G E
    You won't lose your reward

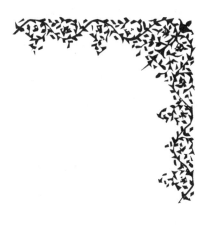

A A A G A
　　In the name of the Lord

G A A A G A
　　You will find your reward

　　Cold water from a cup
　　That is what will fill them up
　　Anyone who gives a cup
　　In the name of the Lord
　　Will not lose his reward

(8va 1st chorus melody)

　　In the name of the Lord
　　You won't lose your reward
　　In the name of the Lord
　　You will find your reward

Edit Draft Moses

5/22/07 6am (The first verse from God to me, the rest is from God to Moses, to Jen, and to everybody. One of my former church friends is named Jen. She has a daughter that won the Miss New York beauty contest. Miss New York sings. Miss New York's boyfriend is a US Marine.)

(Deuteronomy 32)
(this rocks out)

Moses

(from God)

　　Armies that can change the world
　　Don't carry guns or knives
　　Armies that can change the world
　　Are saving people's lives

(Deuteronomy 32: 1, 2)

> Let heaven and earth hear my voice
> The Word like rain that slants
> Like the water of life on tender grass
> Like love on tender plants

(32: 3, 4)

> I will sing out the Name of God
> He is Rock, Maker of Earth
> Sing How "Great Thou Art"
> His perfect creation for sure

(32: 7, 8, 9)

> Remember the old school days
> Consider the generations
> God's portion was His people
> When God gave gifts to nations

(32: 10, 11)

> An Eagle over her offspring
> In the desert He found the best
> He carried them on his wing
> And hovered over His nest

(32: 13, 14)

> He rode on the mountains
> Of honey, oil, milk and wheat
> He ate the fruit of the trees,
> Champagne, cheese and meat

(32: 39)

> He puts to death and brings to life
> Like Him there is no other
> Wounds and heals, yes he does
> From His hand none can deliver

(32: 46, 47)

> Now take these words to heart
> Command children to obey
> These aren't just idle words
> They're life to you today!

Ugly Patterned Notebook

5/26/07 2 pm (Remembering what it felt like to be yelled at and threatened for not turning on the dishwasher, not putting gas in my car when it was below a quarter tank, and generally just for not doing anything perfectly, according to somebody's definition of perfect.)

What Kind

> What kind of life was that?
> Nothing made any sense
> What was I to be doing
> Besides sitting on the fence?
>
> I did the best I could
> I did all I could do
> I gave it all I would
> Nothing seemed to do
>
> I was marking time
> Marching to the drum
> Nothing was really fine
> Everything was just ho hum

I didn't hear God talking
I didn't hear a thing
No music, no poetry
Not any songs to sing

I know you were there
God, I know you never left
It must have been me
That chose to fly the nest.

Maybe it was just a test
To see if I'd stay true
I honored all the promises
That I had made to you

Yes, I see the singers
Falling into line
I see the play on Broadway
And the chorus line

I see the Platinum Albums
Lined up on the walls
I see the souls for Jesus
Saved before they fall

I am good at waiting
I can wait for ever
But what about the people
Who really need to hear

Why can't he get on board?
What is wrong with him?
Why does he have to oppose
Every thought and plan

(male voice)

> I can't take opposition
> I am ready to fight
> My adrenaline is flowing
> It is a full moon night
>
> Bring it on, Whomever
> Dare to cross that spot
> Care to go some rounds?
> Let's see what you've got

(female voice)

> I can forgive whomever
> I know how to do that
> That's easy for a girl
> Who knows just where it's at

> I hate being like this
> I don't want to be mad
> Why can't people be kind
> I am just so sad

Chapter 6

Edit Draft Psalms

5/28/07 9 pm Memorial Day (Big annual party for our family's closest friends at the Lodge today. We have ribs and beverages for two hundred people, boat rides, skiing, and a movie on a huge white tarp. We have a gargantuan fireworks display that two hundred more people watch from their boats. Rich is here lighting off thousands of dollars of fireworks. He says he owns Coljens Lodge. No reason given. Instead of participating, I am taking a break to write.)

There are 150 Psalms in the Bible. I am going to start with the first Psalm and see how far I can get. These aren't necessarily how I feel but I'm going to make an attempt at writing and feeling.

(This is what I see when I look at Psalm 1)

Psalm 1

God's blessing is on those who keep
Company with the sweet,
Who keep his law and His commands
Who follow closely the Son of Man

They are fresh and full of life
Flowing like a running stream
Their pantries overflow with food
Their life is like an evergreen

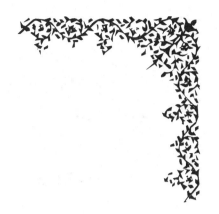

They are sturdy stems of wheat
Standing in the assembly
The Lord spies out their street
And makes them live forever

Edit Draft Psalm 2

5/28/07

Psalm 2

When the rulers of nations
Rile against the King
God redresses their disrespect
And shows His signet ring

Israel is my Holy Ground
The birthplace of My Son
At His request the nations rise
To worship the Holy One

Serve the King with shock and awe
Kiss His feet with trembling
Be blessed, avoid destruction
By hiding in His Holy Wing

(I just deleted a couple of Psalms because I think that the words that I wrote were too simplistic.)

Edit Draft Psalm

5/28/07

Psalm 5

Listen only to me, Lord
Listen in the morning, please
I am waiting patiently
I am on my knees

Show me yourself so I can follow
Show me your righteous ways
Lead me through the enemy lines
Singing all the time

Let all who march behind you
Sing and shout with joy
Raise your shield over their head
Your Spirit they do enjoy

Edit Draft Psalm

5/28/07

Psalm 6

Lord, don't be angry with me
I am weak from the fight
My soul is prayed out, O Lord
How long must I be right?

Turn around and save me Lord
Because you love me still
Please while I am still alive
To praise you like I will

My pillow has been drenched with tears
I cannot see from strain
Away from me those who sin
My weeping like steady rain

The Lord has heard me cry
The Lord has heard my prayer
They will turn and run away
God's mercy with me he shares

Edit Draft Psalm

5/28/07 (This is the last one for tonight.)

Psalm 7

Lord, I hide with you in a cave
Hiding from hungry lions lust
Without you I am lion's prey
Ready to be torn to dust

Wake O Lord and judge my foes
Judge according to my integrity
End the violence of the wicked
And make sure my security

My shield is my God,
Who protects those of His Son
His sword, bow and flaming arrows
Are ready for the evil one

The enemy makes trouble
His child is disillusion
He digs a pit of discontent
And falls into seclusion

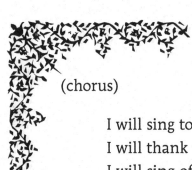

(chorus)

> I will sing to the Lord of Most
> I will thank the Lord of Hosts
> I will sing of the Righteous Name
> The God of earth and heaven's fame

Edit Draft Psalm

5/29/07 (Starting up in the morning...for kids at heart)

Psalm 8 Sticker Stars

> O Lord, your Name is Divine
> On your signature of earth
> You are a crown of splendor
> On the body of the universe
>
> Touching the lips of children
> You have placed your Name
> You close the mouths of evil men
> And those who wish to disgrace
>
> When I gaze into the sky
> At the sticker stars you doled
> The moon you scooped for us
> Like ice cream in a dark bowl
>
> Then I sing

(repeat 1st stanza)

> You made lowly us almost like You
> And gave us royal princely treats
> Furry footstools for our feet
> Songbirds to soothe, fresh fish to eat

(repeat 1st stanza)

Edit Draft Psalms

5/30/07

Psalms 9 & 10 Lion's Teeth

(chorus)

    I will tell You my God
    How I love Your ways
    I will tell of all You have made
    And sing of Your crowning days

    The ungodly trip and fall
    Into the grave they land
    Never to be remembered
    They perish by Your hand

(repeat chorus)

    The victims of the wicked
    Hide behind Your tower
    You hear cries of the afflicted
    Singing praises of your power

    See me behind their iron gates
    Into their netted pit they fall
    Set me free to sing your Name
    Within Jerusalem's walls

    Lord do you see what they do
    The powerful hunt the weak
    They gorge themselves on lies and threats
    They think God will never see

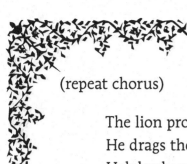

(repeat chorus)

The lion prowls his weakened prey
He drags them off in his teeth
Helplessly crushed under his strength
The lion thinks God will never see

Lord, you do see trouble and grief
You take it into your hands
The victim commits his ways to you
You break the arm of the evil man

(repeat chorus)

Edit Draft Psalm

5/30/07

Psalm 11 Fledgling

The hunter bends his bow
Hiding in the shadows of night
The hunter aims his arrow
At the fledgling in flight

How can you say fly like a bird
To the highest mountain trees
Why say you have heard
That the innocent should flee

The Lord examines wicked men
They'll be under volcano's rain
The Lord observes the heart of them
A desert wind will be their pain

The Lord himself is righteous
Upright men will see His face
The Lord himself loves justice
He faithfully makes a spacious place

(chorus)

Upright men come freely
Upright men come seeking
Upright men come kneeling
Enjoying access to the King

Edit Draft Psalm

5/31/07

Psalm 12 Silver Dross

Help me Lord
I'm all alone
I am in need
You hear my groan

I will stand up for you
The Lord Almighty says
I will protect you from their hand
I will bless, I will bless

The Words of God are perfect
Refined like silver dross
The Words of God are flawless
Protection by the Cross

(I don't know what happened to Psalm 13.)

Edit Draft Psalm 14

6/1/07 evening (Aristotle: A pair of fishermen can net a fish if one plays music and the other dances on deck. I saw this quote on an article in *The Freshwater Angler*, Fishing Tips)

Psalm 14 Walleye on Sevenstrand

Big walleyes are found in stringy strands
That catch your line and foul your lure
You can shake weeds off if they endure
Or reel it in and extract by hand

There's always a better, easier way
Add a short leader of multi-strand
Between line and lure try twelve pound test
Sevenstrand wire works the best

When you feel resistance from the weed
Jerk the rod
Thin wire cuts the weed and it falls
Plus through it, sharp toothed fish can't bite
Sharp toothed fish, like northern pike

Then we'll have walleye from the lake!
Pecan encrusted with lemon sauce
Potatoes, green beans and salad tossed
Cherry topping on New York cheesecake!

(I deleted Psalm 15)

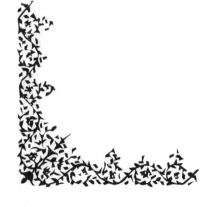

Edit Draft Psalm 16

6/2/07 10 pm

(Now we're really cookin'.)
(African drums 4/4)

African Tribes/Psalm 16

God keep me safe
A pleasant place
Making my dreams
My smiling face

African tribes run their prey till they are weak
They wait in the bush for unsuspecting meek
They chant and drink the blood of their kill
And dance till dawn on a moonlit hill

I am reaching
For Your right hand
Your Son is life
I understand

I am singing
Sweet is my sleep
You counsel me
My life you keep

I know the path
We walk the land
Lasting pleasures
Holding Your hand

Edit Draft Psalm 17

6/5/07 (just past midnight)

Grand Canyon   (I've never been there)

I come into the courtroom   (not been there either)
Before the Godly Judge
Before the Righteous King
I pray thee listen
To my petition
My case is truly just
And not just a clever thing

(chorus)
This is my petition
This is my Godly prayer
Show me the Wonder of the World
The wonderful Love you share   (I've been here)

May my vindication
Come from God
May my interrogation
Come from God
Cross examine me in the night
Search me under the glaring light
My innocence my reputation
May my vindication
Come from God

On the narrow path of rock
Walking upward to the top
From the Canyon wide with heat
Just wide enough for my feet
Pebbles rolling past the rail
My feet have not tripped
My soul has not slipped
You hold me on the trail

(chorus)

This is my petition
This is my great prayer
Show me the Wonder of the World
The wonderful Love You share

You shield me as the center of your eye
From chafing sand and blistering sun
Shade in the canyon of your love
Under powerful wings of Your Holy One

I have no need for pleasures
I gave them all to my sons
The rooms are packed with treasures
When I
When I
When I wake in the morning
Because of the pureness of your grace
When I wake in the morning
I will see Your face
When I wake in the morning
I will see Your Son's face

(repeat chorus)

Edit Draft Psalm 18

6/5/07 5:30- 6:30 pm

(This is me in my Lodge)

Psalm 18: 1-19 NIV

Castle Tsunami/Psalm 18

I am in a castle
Built of precious stone
High up in the tower
The place that I call home

The enemy is circling
With ropes around the base
He's wrapping up the castle
With snares though doors are braced

God was in the highest space
Surrounded by His light
I called to Him from my place
He saved me from my plight

(chorus)

He heard my voice
He heard my fears
He heard my cry
With His very own ears

Then He made an earthquake
That made the mountains rumble
Smoke and coals of fire rose
From the volcano's blackened nose

He pushed aside dark thunderheads
On the backs of angels He flew down
The oceans leapt from their sandy beds
And razed the whitewashed town
Riding angels on a hurricane
On the backs of angels He flew down
He dumped shipyard hulls of frozen rain
That scraped the sky with light
The oceans leapt from their sandy beds
And razed the whitewashed blight

(repeat chorus)

He reached down from within the storm
Caught me from the bottom of the sea
Laid me on the spacious shore
Because He delighted in me

(repeat chorus)

Edit Draft More Psalm 18

6/7/07 9am
(By the way, I have a Black Belt in a secret form of karate, the killing art. That's a secret so don't tell anyone.)
Psalm 18: 20-50

King of the Ring/Psalm 18

I'm stepping through the ropes
Into the fighting ring
There's a great big God
In front of all I bring

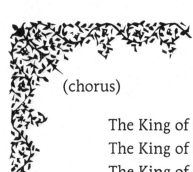

(chorus)

> The King of the ring wins!
> The King of the ring lives!
> The King of the ring sings
> Now and forever we live!

> He's right in front of me
> He knows just how to fight
> My opponent jabbing toward me
> God lands a deadly right

> God looks me over
> The condition of my hands
> The moves I make
> The breath I take
> The trueness of my stance

> God tells me to advance
> He sees my blameless work
> He lifts me in the air
> My heel lands in the eye
> Of the overzealous guy

(chorus)

> The King of the ring wins!
> The King of the ring lives!
> The King of the ring sings
> Now and forever we live!

> God builds my arms with strength
> My feet as fast as fawns
> I can stand on a pinnacle
> And bend a rod of bronze

I take charge in the fight
Not looking back at all
I crushed them into dust
I made every fighter fall

The others ran away in fear
Whining for help from anyone
There was no one to save them
Not even God's own Son

I crushed them under my feet
I poured out their blood
Like flowing mud on the street
God sent me out from the ring

God and I are King of the ring
King in every country
Foreigners cringe in everything
His reputation goes before me

(chorus)

The King of the ring wins!
The King of the ring lives!
The King of the ring sings
Now and forever we live!

Edit Draft Psalm 19

6/8/07 11pm

(You really get to know somebody when you go camping with them. Do you remember when our high school group went camping? If you do, the answer is still no, you cannot sleep with me in the girls' tent.)
(bright & happy)

Camping/Psalm 19

My God threw up a tent in the sky
He likes to camp out on a ridge
He lets the sun stay in the tent
Or lets it roll along a bridge

My God made a law book
Out of the purest gold
And filled it up with honey
That drips out of its folds

I keep this in my backpack
And eat it all the time
This keeps me going on the trail
And makes me feel just fine

My God put songs in my mouth
That taste like fruit and wine
My God put thoughts in my head
That make my bright eyes shine

(chorus, God to me)

Yah, Babe
I hear you lovin' me
I hear the words you sing
I see your lips drippin' honey
I see your eyes and everything

Edit Draft Psalm 21 Wellspring

6/10/07 1 am (Written just after hosting Lindsy Gilligan's huge Sweet Sixteen Party at Coljens Lodge. I also got a free brand new mattress set with delivery for my other lake house on Stephens Road. In the real estate business, other people's divorces and deaths often result in somebody else's gain. No wonder people put realtors in the same category as used car salesmen. Plus, I went to three graduation open house parties and talked to lots of friends! Fun!)

Psalm 21 Wellspring

The strength of the Lord
Is my victory and peace
Unending blessings
And total release

(chorus)

Your presence
Your favor
A wellspring
of blessing

The tower of love
Will not be shaken
Your hand will lay hold of
What has been taken

He captures the crown
Places it on my head
Taken from the enemy
Given to me instead

(repeat chorus)

Edit Draft What It's About Psalm 22

6/13/07 10:45 Psalm 22:1-10 NIV
(country)

What It's About

Why have You forgotten me
Why are You so far away from me
Why can't You hear me sigh
For You every day I cry

But You don't answer me
At night I cry myself to sleep

I know You're there
Everyone knows You're what it's about
I feel as low as a worm
They criticize me like a germ

All my friends trusted you
And you helped them out
They told you their problems
And you said what it was about

Hated by the town
They put me down
And shake their head
In disgust is what they do

They say if I believe in you
Then you should help me out
I know you're there
Everyone knows you're what it's about

Chapter 7

From: AlexaColjen@msn.com
To: JazBachman@msn.com
Attachment Scuba
6/15/07

Here is a funny story about a near death experience I had a few years ago:

Scuba

I had just gotten my Scuba Diving Certificate by passing the written and practical tests. The practical test involved demonstrating knowledge of emergency procedures, such as removing my tank underwater and putting it back on in a simulated entanglement with seaweed. About the only problem I had was wearing enough weights to get to the bottom of the pool. Apparently my little round rear worked as a flotation device.

I could choose the location of the practical testing and I had chosen Cozumel, Mexico. That was going to be much more exciting than the high school pool where the lessons were. In Cozumel, I aced three in-out dives with the nice New York dive master from back home. He acted as my buddy. I passed his test and was officially certified. I had successfully demonstrated that I could buddy breathe, read my gauges, plus, even if I was exhausted and strapped with full gear and heavy weights, I could climb a ladder that was being tossed around in the waves at the back of the boat.

Cozumel diving is current diving. That means that when you enter the water and descend, the undercurrent takes you along at forty or sixty feet below and you don't have to swim. If you don't breathe too fast from getting frightened or swimming hard, there's enough oxygen in your tank for a deep dive and another shallow dive. The boat picks you up forty minutes after each of the dives in the direction of down current.

It was time for me to make my first real dive as Certified Diver. I was standing on the cement shore. About forty people were waiting to board a small dive boat. My New York dive master said, "This is when you practice dives with a real buddy, not me."

I was a little apprehensive as this ocean was a little bigger than the high school pool.

I smiled, "I would like to choose you as my buddy because I want somebody who knows what they're doing."

"Oh no," he said. "I have to stay at the shore to certify the next person, why don't you have your husband for a buddy? He knows what he's doing. He'll stick right with you. Don't worry, he's rescue certified."

Then New York Dive Master took a video of me as I unzipped my ankles and said, "Have fun!"

So, I got on the boat with the group of about forty. There was one dive master onboard who looked like he was about seventeen years old talking to the boat driver. There was another dive master that looked a lot more substantial.

I asked my tall, muscular husband, "Do you think I need a buddy?"

Rich looked at me like I was from another planet.

I put on all my gear, including my heavy weights, while the boat was speeding to the drop-off point. When the engine idled, I let the twenty people in our group jump in ahead of me, including my buddy, Rich, who was the last of them. There was another group sitting behind me on the boat that looked like advanced divers waiting to jump.

I hesitated, jumped in, dropped like a rock to forty feet and breathed in a mouthful plus two lungs full of saltwater. I reached for the mouthpiece end of my air hose, which was floating away above my head. My arm knocked my mask ajar and that filled with saltwater, too. I was very calm. I treaded against the undercurrent and felt my left shoulder for the emergency air supply. I knew I couldn't drop weights and pop to the top because the pressure of ascending from two atmospheres would cause the saltwater to burst my lungs. I couldn't see very well through the flooded mask and I was groping for my emergency air. I looked for Rich, my "buddy", Mr. Rescue Certified. I recognized him floating, then treading. The current had taken him along with the group and he was about a hundred and fifty feet ahead of me.

Teenage Dive Master was right next to me. I grabbed his oxygen out of his mouth. That's the correct emergency procedure and couldn't have been more appropriate. I coughed my lungs into his mouthpiece, purged the water with the little button, and breathed air! I didn't panic and I didn't drown!

I pointed up, signaling Rich that I was getting back on the boat. He signaled that he was going with the group and swam away before they got completely out of sight. He was there for the important business of seeing fish and a half drowned wife wasn't going to sidetrack him.

Once I was on the boat, Teen Master disappeared underwater and the reality that I had just escaped drowning hit me. I started to go into a shock shake. The advanced group was still on the boat and ready to jump into the ocean. Their dive master was huge and muscular with a heavy beard. He said to me with loud Spanish and a lot of pointing that I could tag along with them or stay on the boat with the boat driver. I looked at the big, fat, scary looking driver and he had that look in his eyes. It was the same look you see on the Wanted posters at the post office.

I decided to start putting on my gear again. The Mexican master said with hand motions that he would be my buddy. He wasn't as scary looking as Scary Driver, but almost. One of the advanced divers that spoke English with a Danish accent sat down next to me on the bench. He showed me that the plastic strip that held my air hose onto my mouthpiece had broken. I had almost been a fatality caused by a two-cent piece of plastic. He got me a new plastic strip.

The boat sped to a remote location where the shore was not in sight even if I squinted. Everybody in the advanced group jumped in, one at a time. Mexican Master jumped over the stern into the water. I was still badly shaking but balanced my way on the rocking deck to the back of the boat with the full tank on my back. I looked out over the endless ocean and down over the stern at the waves hitting the ladder.

I heard Scary Driver yelling behind me from the ship's wheel, "Senorita! Senorita!"

I turned around to see Scary Driver with my fins and weight belt in his hands. I had almost jumped in without them. I staggered back to nice Mr. Scary Driver, sat down on a bench right next to him and put them on while still shaking.

Mexican Master was angrily yelling in Spanish with his head above the waves, Arriba! Arriba! Vamanos! Vamanos! By the time I jumped, the whole advanced

group was already out of sight, except for their hired Mexican Master/Guide. He was supposed to be pointing out all the beautiful, colorful underwater sights and getting big tips from the advanced group afterwards. There wasn't anything in sight except water, the bare ocean floor, and a boat prop churning into oblivion. I swam over to Angry Master and kept my eyes riveted on him as we floated along with the current. I didn't want to lose sight of him and become the subject of a "Woman Disappears in Gulf" news story.

He signaled me, "Look at fish", by pointing to his eyes and flapping his hands with thumbs under his armpits. He must have thought he could rescue at least my contribution of a tip. I shook my head, no, and kept floating.

He signaled, "Big shark", and pointed behind my head. I still kept my eyes on him.

He whipped out a diving knife with an eight inch blade and signaled, "Come with me". He swam over to a man-sized black cave opening and pointed to it.

I thought, "Maybe this is going to be my day to die, after all."

In my head, I recited part of the 23rd Psalm, "Yea, though I swim through the valley of the shadow of death, I will fear no evil."

I swam over to the cave because there wasn't any other choice. Angry Master signaled for me to look into the cave. I poked my head into the dark and a humongous green eel with big teeth lunged out and roared at me. Simultaneously, Master Buddy yanked me away from the cave by grabbing my arm. He started laughing through his mouthpiece. After that, I didn't look at anything except his big black wetsuit right next to me. He kept his long knife out and we floated with the current to the end of the trip. He never even tried to stab me.

I was so glad to make the ascent that, even with my mouthpiece, I smiled all the way up through the warm, clear water. When my head broke the surface into the salt air and bright Mexican sunshine, there was the boat with everyone in both groups leaning over the siderail, cheering, clapping, pointing and singing out, "There she is!"

I guess the first group thought I drowned and the advanced group thought I must have been killed by an eel. They were really happy to see me. I was just happy to be alive.

Edit Draft Psalm 23

6/15/07 8:30 pm 6/17/07 10 pm

Filling Me Psalm 23	**Filling Me**
God is my king	(God is my Dive Master)
Find me resting	(See me floating with the current)
He gives me life	(He gives me breath underwater)
Refreshes my wellbeing	(With a rich mix of air)
He revives my soul	(He is the buoyancy for me)
My security	(My compensator)
My prosperity	(My gear, my boat, my team)
Bring honor to my king	(Show God provides generously)
God and I walk together	(God dives with me)
Through fearful places	(Into dark caves of fear)
His authority	(His expertise)
Guides and rescues me	(Points and pulls me from danger)
We share our life	(He's my buddy)
And he honors me	(He lets me choose what to see)
By filling me with His love	(As he fills me with His air)
His promise to me	(He promises always to love me)
Fills me with his love	(With love, He lets me breath His air)
We share our life together	(We dive enjoying below and above)
Through the years forever	(We will always dive sharing love)

Edit Draft Psalm 23

6/15/07 9pm (for kids, I have no idea whose, I just write what I hear.)

I Am a Sheep-Psalm 23

I am a sheep
Hear me bleat bleat bleat
Lie down God says
In the green grass

Come over by the pond
Stay beside the bank
Breathe the fresh air
Be good for my sake

Even when I walk
Into the junior high
You lead me with your stick
You say Here am I

(bridge)

You make me a happy meal
You give me the best place
Puppies and kittens follow me
I like looking at your face

(chorus)

I got a burger at my favorite place
I ordered what I want and got a happy face
Fries on my head and overflowing pop
All that to go and it will never stop

Edit Draft Psalm 25

6/16/07 8 am (This is me today)

All Day Long-Psalm 25

To You O God I give my soul
I am trusting in Your Name
You will never put me to shame
Like those on the devil's roll

My thoughts are of You all day long
Guide my life in faithfulness
Teach me about righteousness
Remind me of Your love song

Forgive my sins of the past
Forget my rebellious days
Remember your loving ways
Your goodness that will last

Lord, always on You are my eyes
Turn and look at me
For I am ill and lonely
The distress of my heart multiplies

(chorus)

Be the Guard of my life
Pluck my sins away
I am within Your gate
My Hope, my Love, my Light

From: Alexa Coljen@msn.com
To: Jaziel Bachman@msn.com
June 16, 2007
Subject: 1974

Attachment 1974

1974

Once upon a time, in a land far, far away, called New York, in a town called Albany, a beautiful, young Princess went into a deep sleep. No one could wake her, no matter how hard they tried. They shook her and kissed her and cried over her but no one could wake her.

She was in another place that had no ceiling and no floor. Sometimes there was only blue sky in the strange place with sounds. Beeping, blipping. Sometimes voices that she didn't recognize. They sounded like murmuring.

After a long time of being in the deep sleep, one day the Princess heard someone say, "What do you want us to do?"

The people sounded as if they were far away from her. So, she didn't wake up for them. The blue sky and strange sounds continued for a long time. She saw two white gauze spirits playing tug of war with her in the blue sky. She looked like a sheet of dark gauze. One spirit pulled east and one spirit pulled west. Both of the spirits pulled as hard as they could. Neither side could win. She felt like she would tear into shreds if either pulled any harder.

One day she heard a woman's voice say, "Do you want us to get Jaziel for you?" She opened her eyes. She looked around the room. She saw a nurse, a man, and a woman. The man looked very worried and he was balding in the front. The woman had salt and pepper hair and she was sitting in a chair next to the bed that the Princess was on.

"Who are they?" the Princess asked the nurse.

"They're your parents," the nurse said.

She thought she might possibly know the woman, but she didn't recognize the man at all.

The woman said, "If Jaz was here, would you eat something?"

The Princess thought, "Jaz is not here. There's no reason to eat."

The woman was crying. "Do you want us to try to find Jaziel for you?" she asked.

The Princess looked at her with the most begging look.

"Yes," said the Princess and she closed her eyes and went back into her deep sleep for a long time.

Then she was in a huge dark rocky cave all by herself. There was fire everywhere. She could hear people screaming and moaning in pain. Then she saw, sitting on a chair in the cave, the man that was supposedly her father. He seemed at home there. She called him a bad name. He didn't know why. He had never tried to harm her. She could tell that the man was especially interested in her by she didn't know why. She didn't think the man was on her side.

Then it got very dark. There was nothing but darkness and some stars. Suddenly, the Princess saw that there was an angel next to her bed. She could see the hospital furniture. She was awake. She could see his tall, glowing, iridescent form with long, feathery wings past his knees. The glow was so bright that she couldn't see his face. She thought, "I'm safe now," and she went back to sleep.

In the morning, she sat up in the hospital bed. "What am I doing here?" she asked the nurse.

"You're very sick. You should lie back down."

"How long have I been here?" she asked politely.

"Three weeks. I'll go get your doctor."

The Princess, being strong willed and opinionated, thought to herself, "I'm fine and they're not keeping me here."

She pulled the IV out of her arm, put her clothes on and walked two miles home. The Princess was never sick again.

THE END

So, Jaz, you question whether our love, when we were in high school, was deeper than most? 1974 is a factual story with no embellishments or exaggerations.

Edit Draft Scarred
(my testimony that Jesus is not dead, he is alive)
6/16/07

Scarred

My life did flow
From His own blood
When I was weak
And nearly died

He sent His Angel
To my side
To show He lives
Although He died

Scars never go away
It's the strongest tissue
That's what they say
The scar tissue of my veins

A reminder that He reigns
Of victory in His Holy Name
Of victory in His Holy Name

Now I'm as strong
As tissue scarred
With His blood inside my veins
Veins that hold the streaming pulse

Of victory in His Holy Name
Of victory in His Holy Name
Of livin' in His Holy Name
Of livin' in His Holy Name

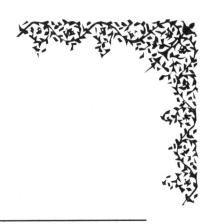

Chapter 8

Edit Draft Hot Soxers

6/17/07 10 pm (Hot Sox is a free Christian basketball day camp. It's for about 200 privileged boys from age six to sixteen. The main thrust is evangelism. The basketball portion and Bible studies are at the home of Guy & Candy Blake, who own Guy Blake Physical Therapy. Guy has several locations and does physical therapy for famous athletes. They have 5 courts in their backyard.)

(About sixty-five Christian basketball coaches, who are mostly pro players and physical therapists, come from all over the country to coach and minister to the boys for a week. About twenty of the coaches stay at Coljens Lodge, for free, for the whole week. I feed them except for the lunches because they're at the camp at lunch time. It's a fun ministry. Every year, one of the nights, I have a big dinner at the Lodge for all of the sixty-five coaches. If they're local, their wives come to the dinner as well. It's a privilege to be a part of this whole minsistry.)

(For the whole week, my house and washing machines are full of very smelly socks and if that is not a privilege, I don't know what is.)

Hot Soxers

God is giving me everything I could possibly want
Except you
I can't believe He would ever withhold anything from me
Except you

He surrounds me with men
That make me feel like a goddess
They trip over each other to wait on me
And tell me that I'm gorgeous

They come from all around the world
Even from Australia
Just to stay with me and eat my food
Even just to "talk to ya"

Rich, handsome, intelligent, delightful men
With beautifully sun toned bods
Men who serve their Lord and country
And dedicate themselves to God

I don't care one bit for them
I don't remember their names
I won't recognize them tomorrow
I think one said it was James

All I can think about is you
I want to tell you what I'm thinking
I want to tell you when I get a sliver
Or a cool breeze makes me shiver

I want to share the sliver of a moon
And when the sunrise shows its crown
I want tell you how the rippled water looks
When the sun is going down

Why does God withhold this from me
Is this how it's going to be
The day you asked how the clouds looked
Was the happiest day there could be

(I have to stop writing now... I'm crying. Maybe I will not be so lonesome in the morning after all these men leave the lodge and go to the day camp.)

114

Edit Draft Angels Unaware

6/18/07 8:30 am (more Hot Sox)
Hebrews 13:2 NIV

Angels Unaware

Don't forget to entertain angels
Though some are unaware
That you sense their very presence
That you see them everywhere

They walk on wooden floors
And lounge up in the loft
They look up at the stars
And keep their voices soft

God sends them to keep you
To protect you from all wrath
To fill the house with power
And keep you on the path

(chorus)

The house is filled with angels
God's messengers and friends
The house is filled with angels
God's everlasting friends

Edit Draft Alexa's Field

6/19/07 Thursday midnight to 12:45 am (My neighbor down the street, Lisa, has been mad at me for a couple weeks for not giving her what she considered to be enough of the donated proceeds for helping with the last Women's Retreat. So, I went over to apologize and gave her more of the money. She wanted it for a trip to Grand Cayman that she said is a "mission" trip with another couple.)

(Hot Sox men are still here.)

Hot Sox Men/Alexa's Field

God, it's amazing how hard you try
These men are spectacular
What kind of a guy
Stays up and cleans
With me at midnight?
And that one that says,
"Tell me about your day"
That blew me away

And the one that looked at my vitamins
And read all the labels
To make sure they wouldn't be fatal.
And the one that said, "What can I do for you?"
And the one that said, "This food is wonderful, thank you."
And the one that said, "You shouldn't have to clean up this,
Let me do it".
And the one that said, "Are you Ok not getting much sleep?"
And the one that said, "Goodnight, Alexa, thanks for everything."
That made me want to sing.

Loving God and people isn't about what you do
Loving God and people is about who you are
It's about just being what God makes you
There isn't any sliding scale that measures how you're doing
It's just a matter of getting up and seeing where got puts you
Like Ruth in the Bible that found herself in a field
That must have been one amazing field

(PS I let the one that stayed up past midnight and cleaned the kitchen with me
listen to your mp3 of Scarred as a reward. He loved it (of course) and said that it
really made him think. I don't know what his name is. He also said it was amazing

how somebody (you) could put that together. He said the song blessed him, so I guess you're now a part of the Hot Sox Ministry, too.)

Edit Draft Cool Sheets

6/20/07 11 pm Psalm 26 (Additional Hot Sox men coming into Coljens Lodge and needing more clean sheets while I'm writing.)

Cool Sheets/Psalm 26

Only looking through Jesus
Does anyone see me as blameless
Jesus is like a linen sheet
That hung between God and me

Jesus is a flowing white linen
That flows in waves when I walk
I kneel to rinse my hands
In a bubbling spring of His talk

I love to walk through the woods
Where God's light falls in shafts
The silence of his truth
The dampness of his laugh

(chorus)

In the crackling of the twigs
And the rustle of the leaves
I hear His voice in the woods
In the spires of the trees

(One Hot Soxer said, "You make me feel like a million bucks and thank you," and gave me a thumbs up. Hmm, I'm not used to hearing kind words like those.)

Edit Draft Under Hand

6/22/07 8:30 am (I'm back from a two hour walk. Do you remember "Rock in a Field" (Rockin' a Field) from January's manila envelope? Well, here's what you would have seen from The Rock very early this morning: The arm and hand of God.)

Under Hand

God is in the sunrise
Its full and blinding light
His arm is stretched across the sky
His fingers long and white
His hand is stretched from east to west

Across the bright blue sky
Resting on a cushion of air
His picture of just why
His protection over my piece of earth (peace)

With me just under his palm
As I walk, He moves with me
Gently singing a psalm

(chorus)

Under His hand
On this green land
He moves with me
I'm under His hand

6/22/07 5pm Psalm 27: 1-6 (I just noticed that this all fits with the beginning of Psalm 27 but hadn't read yet when I wrote these lyrics down.)

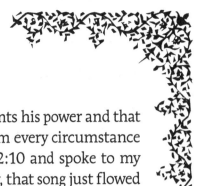

Edit Draft Warm Blanket/Psalm 32

6/23/07 Saturday 8 am (God showed me that his arm represents his power and that it is a symbol of his power to save not just from this life but from every circumstance and to protect from every harm. His Spirit led me to Isaiah 52:10 and spoke to my heart about this song that I had written the day before. Yesterday, that song just flowed out, I could hear God telling me what to write and I could feel the prayers of others.)

6/23/07 10 am (Written after attending the early service at church.)

(country)

Warm Blanket

I am covered with a blanket of wool
The Lord can, but will not see through
When I cower under there my strength leaves
With the heat of His strong arm over me

Then I threw the blanket off of me
And He saw my uncovered skin
I told Him where I had been
And He forgave the guilt of my sin

Let everyone who is like You pray and learn
Let them rest in an upper bedroom
You will lock the door, hanging "Do not disturb"
Your beautiful music will be in bloom

I will tell you about this land
And what I have learned along the way
Don't make me pull you by the hand
Come right to Him, you know the way

Many troubles I have left in the cold
For God's love is like a warm blanket
Be happy with God under His love
Sing while you share it and thank Him

Psalm 27 Reply

How awesome is that? Just like David's Psalms, the first half is the world against you, the second half is about God's favor and victory!

Jaz

6/23/07 So great to hear from you, Jaz. I just looked back and figured out that it has been since April 8th that you have told me anything in my Drafts file. I had not realized that. I feel like you have been communicating with me, nonetheless. Cool.

Edit Draft My Hearer

7/11/07 Tuesday midnight

Psalm 28 (a prayer for power and mercy, a request for deliverance and God's vengeance, worship and then intercession for Christians, the last song in a set encompassing Psalms 23-28)

My Hearer

I'm asking for your power Lord
Don't turn away your head
And if I don't hear from you
I might as well be dead

Hear my cry for mercy Lord
I'm yelling for your help
I'm raising my voice in song
And shouting with a yell

Don't let the wicked have me
Who gossip all day long
Do to them what you will
Repay them for their song

You are the greatest Lord
Because you heard my cries
The Helper in my trials
You are my power and life

(chorus)

You make my heart beat faster
I will thank you all day long
I will worship You my Hearer
And praise you with my song

You are the strength of your beloved
A fortress of strength in Christ the Way
Save your people from the worldly
Blessing them forever and also day by day

(Jaz, if you're reading this, I am going to rent "Brave Heart" tomorrow night. Maybe you want to get the video and watch it at the same time?)

(Last weekend, I hosted the Annual Coljen Family Reunion at the Lodge, even though, technically, I'm not related to the family anymore.)

Edit Draft Complete Thunder

7/18/07 Wed night 11 pm (just finished watching Brave Heart)

I Chronicles 29:10-13

Psalm 29 (a Psalm of completeness in praise of the King of creation. In the Bible, "God's thunderous voice" is used seven times, "God" is used ten times, including the four in the intro and conclusion. In the Old Testament, the number symbolism of seven, ten and four represent completeness. I definitely hear a tripled interpretation.)

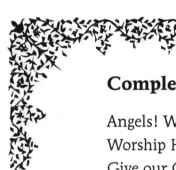

Complete Thunder

Angels! Worship the Holy God!
Worship His Glory and Strength
Give our God His Glory due
In your holy garments of praise

God's thunderous voice is heard
Over the water and waves
God's thunderous voice is heard
With power as we praise

God's thunderous voice is heard
Breaking the strongest trees
God's thunderous voice is heard
Shaking the mountain's knees

God's thunderous voice is heard
As lightening shakes the sand
God's thunderous voice is heard
Twisting the oaks of the land

The land is laid bare and alone
As the Lord speaks from His throne
God's thunderous voice is heard
As God gives strength to His own

Hello Alexa,

Complete awesomeness!

This song is a hit for a praise service. You are so gifted

I got the movie and watched it. If you liked "Brave Heart" you might like to watch "Rob Roy", starring Liam Neeson. I think they use the same kilts, very heroic and romantic.

Jaz

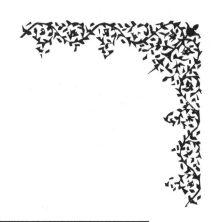

Chapter 9

To: JazielBachman@msn.com
From: AlexaColjen@msn.com
7/21/2007 002100:0000
Subject Slow Saturday Night (with responses)

Dear Alexa, (Dear Jaz,)

(My answers are in parentheses)

So how was the family reunion?

(It was idiotic, 200 people, who have no idea without a name tag what each other's first name is. They all sat with their very immediate families. My kids sat with their dad. I was busy filling the chafing dishes.)

(The good part was that we had a pie auction during it and I raised $300 for cancer research. I love auctions and I know how to get the bid up. The local auctioneers love me and that is usually what I had been doing on Saturdays for the past ten years or so, I mean going to antique auctions.)

(It is nothing for me to hostess around 200 people for the reunion. Over that frazzles me out a little bit.)

(In the early eighties, I read a book on hospitality that said that everything belongs to God and he controls everything, even the house you live in and if the house is a mess when he sends people over or if you don't have the right food, then since it's God's place and his food, that's his business, so relax. Then I got some books about how to keep a place up and another one about how to have food on hand and so on. Then I started small by inviting just a few people over to our small apartment every week. I never got attached to any house after that because I never

felt like it was mine. I could abandoned the Lodge and Stephens House, which is another huge house that we own, any time, and not care one drop.)

I want to change a bit of the wording in 100 Rednecks. I don't speak any Spanish. I'm not sure about any of the Spanish words that you have in it.

(I already put the revision in Drafts while you were writing this letter.)

I want the composition to sound like June Carter Cash, with the improper phrasing, and all that. There is also a verse that is repeated. Do you want it that way or is it an oversight?

(I think that chorus needs to be repeated, but do whatever you think sounds good. I'm not attached to that song or any other song.)

Anyway, you will have it in the Drafts tonight or tomorrow.

(Thanks for using Drafts to communicate. I was in a restaurant with about eight ladies when you called for the very first, and I hope only, time the other day, and I had gone to wash up. When I got back to the table, Shelly, my voice teacher, took one look at me and said, "What happened to you?" I had ridden there with her, so on the way home, I had to tell her that you had called me. Also, I told her about that one day when you came back to high school for me after you had moved away and expected me to ride off into the sunset with you on your motorcycle.)

It's an instrument that you just can't put in a case or buy a new reed for.

(I don't know what you're talking about.)

If we only know each other by what we write, we can always be perfect to each other.

(You're funny. So you think everything you write is perfect? Or maybe you think everything I write is perfect? No. Only Jesus is perfect. We see the imperfections in each other but we realize that this is how God made us. Those are called endearing qualities. Don't ever try to be something you're not. Not for me anyway.)

We can carefully proof everything we write in your Drafts file and delete comments after thinking carefully about what we are saying. No small wonder you think that I can do no wrong. Be careful about that. I don't want you to be disappointed with me.

(It's 12:30 am and I am going to try to get a little sleep. God wants me to write some lyrics about a labyrinth. I'm not sure yet, but the song is about healing and love and the center. You'll be the first to read it. This is going to be exciting to see if he wakes me up with it tonight.)

Bye for now,
Jaz

(See you in the Drafts,)
(Lexa)

Edit Draft A Hundred Rednecks and Me
7/21/07 revision with chords by Jaz

4/15/07 (I'm remembering Sweetest Day five years ago. I went to a gun auction alone. My purchases were the start of my antique gun runnin' to Pennsylvania. I think maybe if I sell my stock of antique guns, it's going to supply money for producing our songs, if we ever get it together.)

(definitely a country ballad)

A Hundred Rednecks and Me

V1   C   F
Was the sweetest day it was, And I was there becuz

                 G   C
They was havin' an auction Of every kind of gun.

        C   F
There was a bonfire blazin', and it was rainin' hard

G   C
The men were thick and smellin' in that Smokey Bandit's yard.

(chorus)

C   F
The auction went forever, I waited there all day

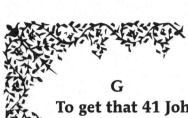

        G   C

To get that 41 Johnson I need that Lord I prayed.

V2 F   C
The sweetest day, that there could ever be

G   C
Biddin' on a Johnson, A hundred rednecks and me.

V3C   F
I was the only woman, that ventured out you see,

G   C
That's how it happened to be, a hundred rednecks and me.

V4   F   C
It was really redneck heaven With all the guns they had,

       G   C
Those Rednecks were a-droolin' the Johnson made them glad.

(chorus here)

V5 C   F
The biddin finally started The other stuff was sold,

       G   C
It was muddy, dark, and rainy, and I was gettin cold.

C   F
The lesser guns were openers, but I had to show my stuff,

G   C
I didn't want the rednecks to think I didn't have enough.

V6 C   F
So I outbid the riffraff on three of the lesser guns,

       G7   C
There on a few of the others I let them have their fun.

(chorus here)

V7 C   F
Finally, the Johnson came up for its bid,

G7   C
I let two rednecks wrangle, just behind the one I hid.

V8 C   F
Then just before the gavel, hit the plywood board,

G7   C
I faced off with a Redneck and said, "Let's do it Lord!"

V9 C   F
The Banderol looked right at me, "A bid from a beauty queen!"

G7   C
I stared him down, without a frown, I raised the bid to seventeen.

(chorus again here)

V10 C   F
He doesn't know who's biddin, he thinks he's biddin to win the gun

G7   C
I kept the score, he can't pay more, I raised the bid to twenty-one

V11 C   F
It got real quiet in redneck haven The yard was thick with smoke

                        G7`   C
There was a faceoff over the gun, this was no redneck joke

V12 C   F
He raised it then not to be outdone He raised it quite a bit,

G   C
I stayed in front on every call I was ready to take a bank account hit

(chorus again here)

V13 C   F
This Johnson must be worth it, 'cordin to redneck haven,

G   C
I took a chance, gave him a glance, and made it twenty-seven.

V14 C   F
Going once, going twice! That's what I came to hear.

G7   C
You got it ma'am the Johnson's yours, you could hear the rednecks cheer

V15 C   F
I wrapped the Johnson in a bag And drove it to Amish land.

G7
The Dutch who knew what this gun was worth, penned me a check for

C
seven grand.

Edit Draft Labyrinth

7/22/07 Sunday 4am (...and now for
something completely Greek to me...)

Labyrinth

To battle the half bull Minotaur   (half-truths from the Devil)
That lives on the isle of Crete   (they look solid, like concrete)
At the center of our love
Where you must kill the beast   (what is troubling you)

Follow the thread
Back to the beginning   (go back to our love, when we met)
Where love and peace
Were without sinning   (just pure love)

You don't need a thread
To keep you
Keep you from getting lost   (you know the way back)
Use the labyrinth   (walk the Way of God toward me)
To keep you
To keep you from
Losing your mind   (we have to do this right, or we'll go crazy)

No false pathways or   (no wrong ways of getting there)
Confusing dead ends   (ways that don't work)
Simple for the neophyte   (I have no idea what that word means)
To find the way to life   (happiness and fullness)

Walk through the labyrinth alone   (I can't do this for you)
Meditate on God's Word
When you get to the center   (when you find the solution)
Remember what you've heard

Leave your troubles at the center   (kill the beast of what is troubling you)
They can't co-exist with love   (that's when you'll have peace)
Your healing is in stability   (we have to resolve things)
Love, joy and peace   (the result)

Edit Draft How we got Labyrinth

July 22ⁿᵈ 2:30 pm

Hi Again Jaz,

How we got the Labyrinth: As I told you, God began speaking to me Friday evening about Labyrinth. I was on the shore by the lake at my Lodge. He told me to rake the sand. I did. It looked like a big crop circle, God said it was a labyrinth. He said to focus on the center. I did that.

God began talking to me, mostly about how much he loves me. He told me that he has given me everything that I could ever want in this life. He said I've flown the sky and dove the ocean. He's given me material possessions, friends, and family. Ministry. That husband was my own choice, he said. He said I'm a selfish brat that needs to learn to be satisfied with only Him. He said he has answered my prayers concerning us as much as he can right now.

Then Saturday morning there was a huge article on the front page of the paper about a labyrinth they had just constructed in Rome. Then when I logged in to my computer at 2 pm, the lead news story was "Crop Circles Real or Hoax?" and the picture looked like a labyrinth. Then, at 4 am, before dawn, the lyrics for Labyrinth woke me up and flowed out, including the interpretation with no stopping and no thinking about it. The whole thing is phenomenal.

3 pm with Love,
Lexa

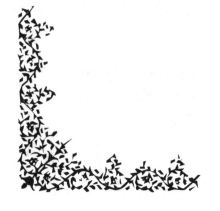

Edit Draft Heavens

7/23/07 8 am

(I'm just loving God. This would be good for congregational worship.)
(poco adagio, sparkling)
Psalm 36:5-10 NIV

Heavens/Psalm 36

O Lord your love reaches to the heavens
To the heights of the furthest deep blue skies
Your holiness like immovable mountains
Your justice is an ocean for our eyes

The weak and poor find safety in the shadow
Of the refuge of your sturdy eagle's wings
The rich and high find safety in the comfort
Of the refuge of your justice in all things

We feast at the banquet of your dwelling
You give us drink from your river of delight
We feast in the light of your presence
With you is the water from the spring of life

(chorus)

Your goodness to all you have created
From the earth to the realms of our dreams
The water from the rivers of your streams
Flows only from the heavens of our God

7/23/07 (Jaz, I think I got the general drift, I mean flow, I mean draft, get it? I might not look at the Psalms for a while. God is blocking that flow and steering my ship toward a different one.)

Chapter 10

Edit Draft Iceberg

5/31/07 (I'm actually reading Pastor Darius Redmond's pre-sermon note written in the bulletin for June 3rd Sermon: Titanic but I see lyrics.)

Iceberg

What lies below the surface
Only God can see
What lives within my heart
Is what is really me

The ship on icy waters
That only God could sink
The ship could cruise forever
Is what the men would think

Listen to the bowmen
Listen to the call
Listen to the steward
Before the fatal fall

A cruise of pompous pleasures
A cruise of unknown fate
A cruise of no remittance
Boarding at the gate

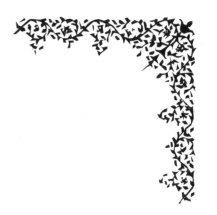

Could it have been avoided
Can we go back in time
Is destiny our future
Does God control our lives

The choices that we make
The promises we take
The words of now and here
The Word to us is clear

Edit Draft My Titanic

6/4/07 2:30 am (From Pastor Darius Redmond's Sermon: "Titanic". I was writing these words into a notebook while he was preaching. I heard the lyrics and wrote them down right before he said the sentences with the same ideas and most of the same words. It was like his sentences were an instant replay. It just means that the Spirit of God was acting.)

My Titanic

An iceberg disrupted the trip
Literally sank the ship
We can listen and be warned
Not shipwrecked by the storms

(chorus)

We need to understand
I am just a man
There was pride
That day and time

Nine eleven's twins
The symbol and the sign
Of our place and time
Representing freedom

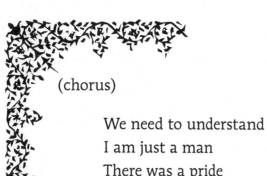

(chorus)

> We need to understand
> I am just a man
> There was a pride
> That day and time

(bridge)

> The minute that we test
> The words, "In God We Trust"
> We're in danger as a country
> We're in danger as a family

(chorus)

> We need to understand
> I am just a man
> There was pride
> That day and time

Edit Draft Tender Heart

6/6/07 7am (From God to you, Jaz. You are supposed to compose some music for this, fairly quickly, and then get it down to Steve Ashton in Nashville, who will produce it. He just needs you to sing how it goes. I know you have the melody because I hear you singing it. Steve Ashton is somebody I met when I went with Jen to watch her daughter compete in the Miss America Pageant. Say the word and I will get you his email address.)

Isaiah 40:1-5 NIV
(style: pop rock)

Tender Heart

Dear Tender Heart,
Your slavery is freed
You have already received
Twice the pain
For which Jesus did bleed

You see Who is coming
Make a straight line
For the Word to run
Fill in the low times
Cut through the highs
Make the rough times
Easy for everyone

(chorus)

Then the Spirit will be seen
By every one
Then the Spirit will be seen
By every son

(bridge)

Sing out
Sing loud
What shall
I sing

All men die like the grass
Just like a flower they die
My life comes from God's own breath
Only the Word of God
Will keep me fresh
Only the words of God
Live forever

Edit Draft Ready for the Date

6/6/07 2 pm (I was making a crab salad sandwich lunch for myself in the Lodge kitchen. I stopped making the sandwich and wrote down the words for this. I was also thinking about a possibility. That is the possibility of you coming to Rome to get me and whether I would really be ready to leave if that were to occur.)

(easy listening, moderato)

Ready for the Date

When Christ comes for coffee
Will you be ready to go
Will you be drinking your latte
Or on your way to a show

(chorus)

I want to be waiting
Right by the front door
Ready to leave
With Him evermore

When Christ comes to get you
Will you have to say bye
Will you have to leave a party
Or cut short a long drive

(bridge)

I want to be ready
When Christ picks me up
I want to be dressed,
With full hair and make up

(chorus)

> I want to be waiting
> Right by the front door
> Ready to leave
> With Him evermore
>
> When He comes to get you
> Will you say it's too soon
> Will you say He should wait
> Till December or June

(repeat chorus)

Edit Draft Pre-Jonah

6/7/07 10pm (Written while looking at the church bulletin. Pastor Darius Redmond's pre-sermon note for June 14th sermon: "Jonah")

(lightly)

Pre-Jonah

> God says it's time to pack
> Time to get on the ship
> Drop the things from your back
> Get ready for your trip
>
> Where on earth can I hide
> There's nowhere I can go
> I would just like to stowaway
> Where no one will ever know

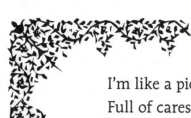

I'm like a piece of baggage
Full of cares and woes
Where can I keep my troubles
Whenever my ship goes

If I take them with me
They'll effect everyone in sight
They'll shipwreck all the sailors
And cause a storm in the night

They'll throw me off the sailboat
They'll feed me to the sea
They'll try to save their own lives
They won't care a bit for me

Good thing God's my maker
And the maker of the sea
Let them throw me in it
He'll take good care of me

I'll leave all my troubles
In the belly of a whale
That will make him really sick
Let him cry and fail

Then I'll end up on the shore
Of a tropical island breeze
God will place me on the beach
Just as happy as you please

(chorus as often as needed)
I'll leave all my baggage
In the belly of a whale
I'll bask in the Son shine
Of an island when we sail

138

Edit Draft Martyrs

6/7/07 11 pm (I was thinking about Hebrews 12: 1-6 NIV)
(this rocks)

Martyrs

A great crowd of martyrs
Looking down on us
Abraham, Abel and Enoch
Noah, Jacob and Isaac
Gideon, Samson and Joseph
David, Samuel and Moses
Not one received the promise
Of what was promised to us

The world was not worthy of them
Or of the love of God's Son
And we are not worthy either
Of the love He's bestowed on us

Let us run with determination
The course marked out for us
Let us fix our eyes on Jesus
Who endured our sin on the cross

(chorus)

Keep your courage in the battle
Take your pain as God's own Son
Holiness and peace are your reward
You are one of God's own sons

Edit Draft Krump Morph

6/8/07 10pm (I wrote this while watching an online video news clip about King Krump, a street dancer.)

(rap)

Krump Morph

I'm gonna morph myself
I gon be a krump dancer
Like the King krumper
I gon be the buck krumper
Bring yo chest pops
An yo arm swings
Bring yo buck syncs
An yo lock pops
I gettin amped jus thinkin bout it
Jesus yo can do anything

Can yo turn me to a buck krumper
I goin to the battle zone
Time fo my session
No mo messin
Bring it on homey
This life is fo me
Like in Papua New Guinea
Yo can come an see me
I'm takin the love down
I'm takin it wit me

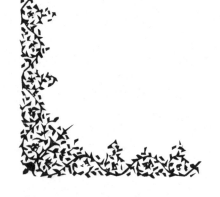

(chorus)

> I said I'm gonna rep Jesus
> Cause it's 'bout the lovin'
> Ain no mo misbehavin'
> Gon be in yo direction
> An gon be about perfection
> Gon be a krump dance
> Gon be gettin amped

Chapter 11

Edit Draft How To

6/11/07 5 am
(Jaz, this is your life, I heard this.)

How to Disappear

My life is like a beautiful kite
Flying way, way, way up high
I want to let go of the string
Watch it disappear in the sky

(chorus)

Flying, soaring
Into the clear blue sky
The angels are cheering for me
My spirit is soaring high

Don't come crashing down
Beautiful fragile life
Don't plummet to the ground
Stay on your windy flight

Soar up to the burning sun
Feel its marvelous heat
Don't get caught up in a tree
Your flight is something sweet

Just let Jesus fly your kite
Just let go of the little string
Watch it dip and rise and fly
He's the Master of Everything

(repeat chorus)

Edit Draft Dispatcher

6/11/07 6 am (I was awakened early with a vision of a truck dispatcher and the words. Does this mean anything to you?)

Dispatcher

There's a gray haired man
Giving you a jacket
It's navy blue with a collar
There's a blue shirt with it

Jesus is the head dispatcher
On the truckin' line
He tells you where to go
And when to leave on time

Tune in to his voice
When you're on the line
Listen when he says
Breaker break one nine

I'll be waiting for you
Waiting for your call
I hope you got a phone
And the wherewithal

(chorus)

> I'll be waiting right here
> When you're on the truckin' line
> I'll be waiting right here
> Just waiting for our time

Alexa,

I usually drive a rig as my summer job.

Jaz

Breaker break one nine Jazz Man, this here's Flaky Pastry, you still got the pedal to the metal? Over.

Edit Draft Selling

(I am taking all my nice business suits to the consignment store.)
6/13/07 7:30 am Luke 18:22 NIV

Selling Treasures

> The camel is selling its saddle
> To buy water for the poor
> All the treasures it used to wear
> Are going out the door
>
> All of the treasures of heaven
> Love, life, joy and peace
> Are being stored in a barrel
> To be poured out at a feast
>
> Silver, gold and diamonds
> Are rolling down the street
> Brilliant songs of the future
> Will be the poor's relief

(chorus)

> Sell your treasures
> For the poor
> Life with God
> Is your reward

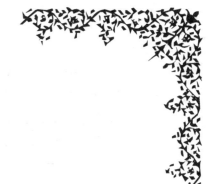

6/13/07

Dear Pink,

Other than his little response to Dispatcher, Jaz hasn't responded to Selling Treasures, or any other Draft for a good long while. It has not been as long as thirty-five years but a while. I wonder what his life is really like?

Edit Draft No Reply

6/13/07 9 pm (I took a two hour walk. I got away from the computer. Then I went back into my home office at the Lodge and guess what? Still nothing from Jaz Bachman that would rock my boat or flip me out of it.)

(style: Red Hot Chili Peppers)

No Reply

> I don't know what no reply means
> But here's what I have seen
> I cut a new trail through the woods
> Through the poison ivy and the snakes
> I'm getting to the running stream
> I don't care what it takes

I found some wildflowers on the path
The most royal purple you've ever seen
They looked like thistles without the thorns
They smelled like flowers in a dream
Like some kind of soap and old spice
I think you know what I mean

Then a red winged blackbird
Decided to be my friend
He followed me as I walked
Then waited till I caught up again
And a single cottontail
Did the same thing as well

Then a single dandelion wish
Followed me all the way back
Riding on the current of my wind wash
Lofting in the air the whole trip
I don't know what this is all about
But I sure would like to find out

(chorus)

What does it mean when there's no reply
Does it mean yes or no
Maybe it means maybe so
Or maybe the message didn't go
Maybe you just don't know
This would be a Peppers song if it had snow

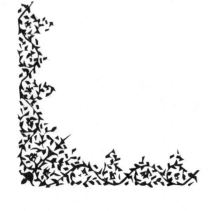

Edit Draft Melchizedek

6/13/07 10pm *Psalm 110* (I wonder what copious means.)

Melchizedek

We know Who's ahead of who
And Who is sitting where
And Who has influence in the world
And Who is prominent there

Under the robes
Of a beautiful queen
Each and every morning
Your virile Princes hold high the lamp
Streaming forthright into the camp
Each and every dawning
As copious as the dew

(chorus)

You are a Priest forever
A Prince of the living God
You are a Priest forever
A Prince of the living God

You will crush the mortal grapes of wrath
And heap dead brush in a flame
You will drink from a brook along the path
And have renewed strength and fame

Edit Draft Trombone Dream

6/14/07 5 am (The whole thing is a dream that woke me up.)

Trombone Dream

You're lying in your trombone case (I don't know how you fit in there)
And I'm thinking (in the dream)
It's shaped like a horrible coffin (like in an old horror movie and it hurts)
Your slide is stuck (you are stuck)
It's rusted shut (you want to live but you can't)
You can only play one thing (tradition)

And then the conductor begins to (God)
speak
He says you need a ton of oil (Holy Spirit)
You need this for a week (to get you through the week)
Everyone else is practicing (it seems like everybody else is OK)
The concert is in a week (not sure)
Some kind of symphony (the whole orchestra, everybody needs you)
Music all on sheets (the Bible)

It's a brass sectional (your focus on anything impure)
There aren't any winds (missing me)
What kind of music is this (I'm thinking I don't understand everything)

I beg you to just (in the dream)
Come out of the case (I want you to be happy)
How can you fit (I'm wondering)
You're in the orchestra pit (It's depressing)

To be continued...

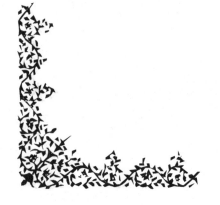

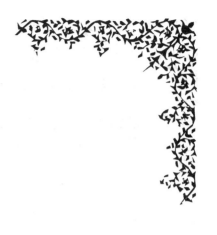

Edit Draft Delete

6/16/07 11pm (I need to delete some whole songs after I write them.)

Delete

I'm having to delete everything I write
Somebody should invent some invisible type
You could only see it with special glasses
That would only work if I'm where your love is

Or maybe I'll start using mental telepathy
Brain waves coming at half past three
Make sure your brain isn't stuck in a dream
Or thinking about some kind of rocky road ice cream

Maybe I'll just write whatever I like
And scare the pants off everybody in sight
Everybody's eyes can get as big as sin
Their jaws can drop open and flies can fly in

I'll have to write stuff in secret notebooks
Volumes and box loads of hot popping kernels
Dripping with butter if you know what I mean
And filled gooey with meringue on banana cream

Now this needs a chorus
One that's just for us
Delete de delete
Delete de delete us

Edit Draft Kindly

6/15/07 8:00am (on the way to Albany for a State
of New York Real Estate Broker Meeting)

Luke 1: 5-9 NIV

Kindly

It's His grace that will sustain you
The Word of God that will train you
Will make you be productive
And show you what love is

Please add to your faith: Goodness
And the knowledge of who heals us
Self-control from Him who shields us
And may you persevere

May you find the way of Goodness
Godliness unlocks your kindness
And kindness is the way to love
Kindly is how we love

He gave His best to woo us
With His kindness God pursued us
He gave to us His precious Son
He wanted to pursue our love

See this and see the future
See life here and ever after
See the coming of our rapture
See that kindness is the way to love

See that kindness is the road to love
See that kindly is the way to love

Edit Draft Dark Womb & Light in the Wilderness

6/24/07 Sunday 10:30 pm

(Sometimes church messes me up. It's like, I KNOW what God told me, showed me, and let me see. Then why do I say to myself, I wonder if I should ... whatever? Here's Pastor Redmond: "3 questions: What am I thinking about? What am I doing? What am I feeling?")

(Then comes the typical Christian messed up response: I shouldn't be thinking, doing, feeling whatever. Mind, will and emotions are at peace when we remember that verse: "Be anxious for nothing but in all things with prayer and thanksgiving, let your requests be known unto God and the peace that passes understanding will guard your heart and mind forever.")

It's about being honest with God and realizing that He is on your side even when you don't think or feel like you're on His.

Then while waiting for anybody to show up at my listing's Open House today, I was reading in Stormie O'Martian, Finding Peace for Your Heart: Seven things that are always true about me:

1) I'm a child of God, he gives me every good thing John 1:12
2) I have a God ordained purpose 1 Cor 2:9
3) I have a specific calling 1 Cor 7:24
4) I am never alone because God is with me Mat 28:20
5) I am not forgotten Rom 11:12
6) I am loved John 15:9
7) I win over bad whatever Rom 8:37

(I am going to make a song about Isaiah 43:19 that I will call Road in the Wilderness)
8 pm (Jeremiah 1:5)
(country)

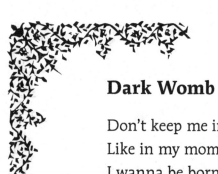

Dark Womb

Don't keep me in the dark
Like in my momma's womb
I wanna be born into the light
I wanna get born real soon

Before you formed me as a youth
You knew I was becuz
Before you formed me in the womb
You knew just who I was

Now don't keep me in the dark
Where I don't know what is
Give me light and give me life
I don't like suffering

I don't like the hurt and pain
I don't like nowhere to go
I don't like being told today
Don't let your feelings show

I wanna see the light of day
I wanna know there's room for me
I wanna know I can leave the place
Where there's nothing I can see

I wanna be born
I wanna be free
I need the light
I wanna see

8:15 pm Jeremiah 1:5 Isaiah 43:19

(Who's your Daddy? It's a rap song about Jesus, so wrap it up good.)

152

Light in the Wilderness

You are a light in the wilderness
The almond on a tree
The inspiration of a song
And the apple meant to be

The words of God are in your mouth
He has touched your lips with fire
The oil of life is on your head
To love the Lord is your desire
You are loved by the living God
Who called you from your home
To say the Word with fire and light
With power from the throne

(chorus)

Firelight and burning desire
To light the road and way
Firelight and burning desire
To light the nations' way

Edit Draft Our Fortune
June 27, 2007 8:30 am
Jeremiah Chapter 33: 1-11 (I'm reading my Bible.)

Our Fortune

While we were still in the prison of our lives
God spoke to me again through His Word and Spirit
God who spoke and the earth was created, it could hear it
God who spoke and set the earth in the universe of stars in the sky
Jehovah is His name. Ask me and I will answer you He said
And tell you the answer to why. And tell you the answer to why

You have torn down your house to protect my love
And for I time you won't be able to find Me ... find Me
But then I will bring overflowing peace and security
To you and the people that love Me ... love Me ... love Me
I will put the house of your love back together as when you were young
I will forgive you for being anxious and not trusting Me ... trust Me

You will bring Joy praise and honor to my Name
When people hear of the love I have restored to you
When they hear of all the good things I am going to do
They will shake with joyful laughter and praise for Me
They will burst into joyful song and praise Me ... Praise Me
When they see the riches, health and peace I will restore to you

You see this is an empty place where no men live or stay
Yet the whole village will hear the sound of praise, praises for my Name
Our voices will be raised in joyful songs of newlyweds
Wearing white clothing of the Lamb ... Wearing garments of the Lamb
We will bring the sacrifice of Praise to the house the Lord restores
Our songs will fill the sanctuary of His house forevermore

This will be our song:

Give thanks to the Lord Almighty
He is so good to give us this
The pleasure of His voice
The sweetness of his kiss
His love that lasts forever
Can't make it disappear
Time cannot erase it
Or even a flood of fear
The love He has for us
We have for each other
So that we could see
So that we could feel
That nothing could erase it
Love is from the Lord
Nothing can replace it

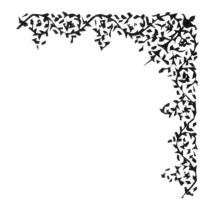

Love for each other or
The love of the Lord
It is a fortune that will
Always be restored

6/28/07 9 am

Good Morning Pink Notebook,

This morning (5 am) I read my Bible and prayed that God would give J to me. How will you do that God? I don't want to be shunned as a divorced woman. I don't want to be thought of as one that only cares about wanting to be with a man. Then I went back to bed instead of writing down a song and actually fell asleep and dreamed J's life.

I dreamt everything about him that I had missed in the thirty-five years since I had last seen him. He never told me any of those things. I saw everywhere that he had ever been in the thirty-five years. I saw him getting music training in old stone buildings at a University. I saw him at an end times camp, with pick-up trucks parked and trees burning. I saw him with women that were part of his life. I don't know if it was everything, but it was plenty for me.

Edit Draft God is brilliant

Hello Jaz,

I hope you are reading Drafts because I have to tell you this:

God is wonderful and I love Him.

This morning, after I wrote out a dream, I was thinking, "Am I completely crazy or totally sane?" Like, am I living in the spiritual realm and really hearing from God or just imagining everything? So I asked God.

Then I was compelled to go to my real estate brokerage. Lots of circumstances occurred that would take a long time to write out. Suffice it to say that I hadn't scheduled myself to be at the office but I ended up there with my hair in a wet pony tail.

Anyway, immediately, in walked a graying couple. That is highly unusual because we don't get a lot of walk-ins without appointments, graying or otherwise. They told the receptionist that they had to talk to me and only me. They must have seen my ads as being the top Realtor for lake properties or something.

They told me that they're looking for a lake house. I sensed God telling me to ask them how long they'd been married. That was not a typical question that Realtors ask. It is against the law to discriminate on the basis of marital status so we stay entirely clear of the topic, at first, until it's time to sign an offer. I have even found houses for people who weren't legally married but were wearing wedding rings. One couple was wearing rings but married to other people! You never know what is real and true with people.

So, here's what they told me: They were high school sweethearts thirty-five years ago, were both previously divorced, and have seven grown children (just like, combined, you and I have), and most importantly, they are very, very happily married.

I just stared at them.

They said, "Aren't you going to look on the computer for a house for us?"

Love,
Lexa

Edit Draft Commit

Hello Jaz,

Right now there is a word rattling around in my head, (oh, wait, that implies that there is some space in my head). Ok, there is a word trying to soak into my brain. It is that word commit. That is a huge word with lots of meanings. Here's what I researched online today: "comes from the Hebrew root galal, which could be rendered as 'roll away'."

How about this: Josh 5:9 "This day have I rolled away (galal) the reproach of Egypt (symbol of sin) from off you" and the Lord named the place "Gilgal" which is a word-play meaning a wheel or "rolling away". In love, God rolls away the reproach of our sins. Get this: Gillgale is what God told me to name the subdivision development where the Lodge is. That is a big long story, but I named

it Gillgale and it's in big gold letters on two stone walls at the entrance to the subdivison.

Then there is the meaning of commit meaning to be doing something. Perpetrating. Like committing a crime. Bad connotation.

Commit is a very interesting word and I have a feeling that this song might end up in a red as molten lava notebook.

Well, if I ever get to see you, I will be glad to show you all the notebooks of varying degrees of hotness.

A & F ("Always & Forever"),
Lexa

Edit Draft Commit

July 1, 2007 (All very hot and cold night long I haven't gotten any sleep whatsoever but it only took me five minutes to write this at **8 am.**)
(Not too seriously country but you never know.)

Commit Me

(chorus)

> Yes it's true I can't commit
> So just commit me
> I guess that's it
> I'm crazy in love
>
> Lord knows I can't do what I should
> Can't get it right and can't be good
>
> When your truck comes by   (you could take out this line)
> I'll be the one standin' in the road
> Don't run me over
> Just slow it down good
> I'm gonna jump on the hood

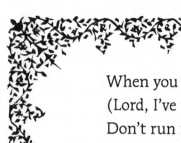

When you drive by
(Lord, I've tried to be good)
Don't run me over
I'll just ride on the hood

(chorus)

Yes it's true I can't commit
So just commit me
I guess that's it
I'm crazy in love

I'll be the one with my
Lunch in a sack
Standin' in the road
With the clothes on my back

(chorus)

Yes it's true I can't commit
So just commit me
I guess that's it
I'm crazy in love

I'll be the one
Standin' in the road
With my lunch in a sack
And my stuff in a backpack

I'm goin with you
Whatever it takes
Don't make me crazy
Before my nerve breaks

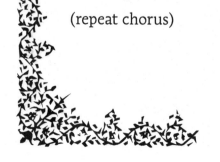

(repeat chorus)

Edit Draft Chicken with stuff(ing)

7/6/07 9 am

Good morning Jazz Man,

I am cooking enough chicken with stuffing to feed an army. The Lodge is always filled with some kind of a gathering. Either Lance is having his fraternity over or Josh is having a mud wrestling party. There is some kind of a secret meeting upstairs where a bunch of Lance's football player buddies were memorizing something or other. I think they are all in the same fraternity as Lance.

Josh used the bobcat to dig a "pond" behind the lodge and filled it with the garden hose. There are a lot of muddy girls running through the lodge and the showers are all running. Josh just came into the kitchen to tell me that the girls are into it too much and are trying to strangle each other in the mud. I told him to go get the football guys to pull them apart.

I have printed off all the songs since January except the secret notebook ones. There are about 250 songs. I'm in the middle of putting them in alphabetical order and sending them to the US Copyright office as: "Lyrics Anonymous V January-June 2007 with music to be added later". This is taking a few weeks to accomplish but I'm almost done. The V is for Victory!

I was afraid to compile everything. I don't know if anybody will ever listen to any of the songs. If nothing else, I guess if I shred all the copies it could make good stuffing for something, but not the chickens.

Chapter 12

Edit Draft Fire

7/7/07 name revised to Money
4/11/07 1 am-3 am
(Written from an AP news story that I was looking at online: "Fire Destroys Longtime Johnny Cash Home" April 10, 2007. I printed it and wrote from the copy.)

Money

Money was his God
He lived beside the lake
A showcase that it was
It was a big mistake

Tuesday's viscous child
Flaming without cause
Destroyed the famous home
Where a "Ring of Fire" was

(refrain)

At the dawn of rock n' roll
He began to Walk the Line
But it held him in a Prison
That burned for all of time

He entertained elite
Impressed them with the best
Royalty and fantasy
Put him to the test

Johnny and his wife
With money in her name
Lived in the lucky house
Till death had made its claim

(repeat refrain)

Nine eleven's heroes
Laid it on the line
One was hurt by fire
But made it out on time

Aspirations landed
Many often times
Jesus tried to save him
"Lonely Rivers" flowed beside

The good Lord points his finger
A "Ring of Fire" from the sky
Lands on whom He chooses
Not anyone nearby

When money picks its victim
Love overpowers all
The family of the owner
Listens to the call

The culture of our system
Worships stone and wood
You'd think he'd lost a marble
The way the building looked

Merry Christmas, Easter
Happy New Year Tea
Reunion, Graduation
And Cash's homes were three

The only house they lived in
The only home they knew
They lived and sang and tried there
Until their lives were through

They did preserve the structure
They did the best they could
How were they to imagine
What they did would burn the wood

(refrain)

At the dawn of rock n' roll
He began to "Walk the Line"
And it held him in a "Prison"
That burned for all of time.

Edit Draft Fireball

7/9/07 1 am (I was looking at an online news story, MSN News June 27, 2007 "Crater Could Solve 1908 Tunguska Meteor Mystery", SPACE.com). I saved this article because I saw it as a song and this was the first chance I had to write it.

(Triple interpretation: Spiritually, emotionally, physically)

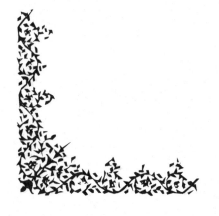

Fireball

(intro)

In late June a hundred years ago,

A fireball exploded
Above a remote forest of confusion
The meteor caused devastation
Razing the woods with degradation

Stargazers are left to guess
Whether if being asteroid or comet
Would make future difference
To avoid calamity on it

A deep lake in the epicenter
Is now called a smoking gun
Researchers of our day found
Seismic waves reflecting at the bottom

Nobody has ever found this before
The waves of the lake
Are explained as a low velocity
Impact crater and by the shape

To really find out if this is impact
We need a core ten meters deep
Where part of the fireball lies
That is the same as thirty-five feet

(chorus)

Fireball from the sky
Creating a lake of waves
Who can know the mystery
Of just how Jesus saves

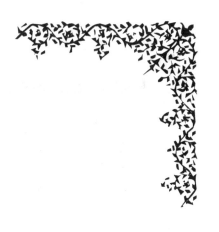

Edit Draft Ezekiel

7/10/07 noon (I just got back to the Lodge from the Tuesday Bible Study. Bertrande Solidino, counselor, speaker, nurse, leads about 100 women every week. We are from many denominations. She is a gifted teacher. She runs a free counseling center in the building where we meet. The study starts with singing, led by the secretaries. These singers are the same women that lead the singing at the Women's Retreats that I host at Coljens Lodge.)

(God is telling me that I'm supposed to share these verses/songs with you which I wrote down as Bertie was teaching and that He's bringing our relationship into holiness.)

(From God to you)

Ezekiel

Even in a hard place
Does God forsake His people
He does not

Hear the Word of the Lord
His messengers speak to us
When He does not

Eat the Words of life
They are as sweet as honey

(Eze 1:4 a description of you)
A windstorm coming from the north (powerfully filled with the Spirit)
Surrounded by brilliant Light (glowing with the love of God)
Fire and molten silver (passionate and purified holy, valuable)
The appearance of a Man of Life (God sees you as if and so do I)

11:1 (God to you)
Prophecy son of man (you)
At the entrance, at the gate (our ministry)
Where the leaders gather and plan (our churches)
Prophecy to save this land (America)

164

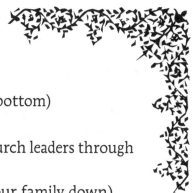

18:3

The parents have eaten sour grapes	(yours, see note at bottom)
And the children pucker at the taste	(their bitterness)
Speak to the leaders	(prophecy to the church leaders through song)
Who cared for themselves	(who let you and your family down)
When the enemy laid in wait	(and let Satan gain a foothold)

34:11-16

(what you are to prophecy from God to the church leaders through music)

I will rescue them	(God will rescue those who have turned away)
From clouds of darkness	(From uncertainty and depression)
The sleek and strong I will destroy	(Who are only intent on themselves)
Like a shepherd tends his sheep	(we who depend on God)
I will bring back the strays	(God will)
And they will graze the good land	(peace and prosperity)
For all of my days	(forever)

37:1-4

Can these dry bones live?	(depressed in the trombone case)
Oh God only you can know	(God has all the answers)
Prophecy over these bones	(speak the Word to your own self)
Come four winds	(all the power of God)
So these bones can breathe again	(the Spirit of God in you and out through you)

(As for that line about the parents: I just want to write a letter to your mom thanking her for giving you birth and to both of them for raising you and yes, even for taking you away to Canada after high school and I'm crying now.)

Edit Draft Surfing

7/14/07 3 am (I always round up the minutes and put the time on when I finish, it's really **2:54 am.** Surfing the Net, get it?)

Surfer

I am

Ridin the biggest wildest wave there ever was (your and/or Jesus' love)

I'm shootin the curl at Weimei (I've been there and it's awesome)

And I'm ridin it all the way to shore (till we're together)

I'm gonna wait till the swell is just right (God's timing)

Not that one, not that one, not that one (bad choices)

Then swim, swim, swim hard (and work hard in the Spirit)

Pop up on my board and ride! (then enjoy it, uprightness)

Ride the biggest wildest wave there ever was

And balance! (everything will be perfect)

Don't let that wave throw you down! (don't let circumstances throw you off)

You'll hit the coral man and it's shallow here! (being together the selfish or wrong way)

You'll bleed! (it would hurt you!)

So stay on your board (stay on God's way)

And ride till that tall wave takes you all the way to shore. (How tall are you?)

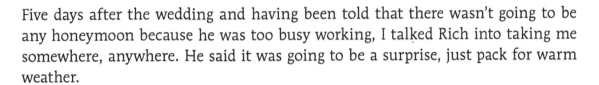

Edit Draft 1980 Honeymoon

7/18/07 11 pm

1980

Five days after the wedding and having been told that there wasn't going to be any honeymoon because he was too busy working, I talked Rich into taking me somewhere, anywhere. He said it was going to be a surprise, just pack for warm weather.

So we had gotten in one of his airplanes with all our big luggage and Rich's fancy cameras and he had piloted us to a little airport outside of Fort Lauderdale, Florida. When we got to that small FBO, the manager asked where we were going to stay. Rich said he didn't know. The manager gave us a phone book, told us good luck, and that it was night time, please lock it when we leave.

We used the desk phone to call every hotel and motel within an hour's drive of Fort Lauderdale. Finally, one place said they had a vacancy and it was only fifty dollars. It was called the Wild Gardenia Miami. That sounded nice. Yippee! It was very late and we were tired. We called a taxi.

The driver dropped us off in the dark, on a sidewalk, along with four large suitcases. Rich was sporting his three large camera bags. We looked around at the dingy, trashy deserted area of Miami where all the buildings formed the block. Rich was right, this was a surprise. The hotel was a two story brick building with no windows and a plywood door. Rich knocked on the door as the cab sped out of sight on the empty street.

A sliding square peep hole opened and a gruff voice ordered, "Show me your police ID".

Rich shouted that he only had a driver's license, which he held over the square.

The door opened. There were five really built Hispanic guys sitting in a small circle on metal folding chairs. They were smoking and watching a little black and white TV. They each had a pack of cigarettes rolled into their T-shirt sleeve. They all turned their necks and stared at the camera bags.

"That's fifty bucks," the guy said that had opened the door. He was a white version of the Hispanic guys.

Rich gave him a hundred dollar bill. Door Guy went behind a makeshift wooden counter and held the bill up to a light bulb hanging from the ceiling. Then he rubbed it on a piece of paper. (Real money leaves ink.)

Tears started to leak out of my eyes.

Door Guy didn't give Rich any change but said loudly to the Hispanics, "Take her up and show her the room."

Two T-shirted guys jumped up, grabbed the cameras and stomped up the narrow staircase. We grabbed our luggage and followed them up into the dimly lit second floor.

In the second floor hallway, we passed a courtyard below that was overgrown with tall weeds. The railings looked like iron bars. T-shirt Guys dropped the bags and put out their hands for tips. Rich opened his wallet and gave them whatever was in there and they ran down the stairs. Then Rich put the key in a flimsy wood door and opened it. The door hit the bed. There was only enough room for a bed in there because this place was a converted jail, only not too converted.

I said quietly with tears, "Rich, I can't stay here."

"Shut up! You'll be OK. There's no other place to stay."

"Please. I can't stay here. Please get me out of here."

"OK, OK, you're the one that wanted a honeymoon."

So we dragged everything back down the stairs and Rich told Door Guy that we wanted our money back. Door Guy said, "Don't you like it here in Little Havana?" He said that because of a huge convention, there wasn't anywhere else to stay in Miami, Fort Lauderdale or nearby. He gave back only a fifty dollar bill. He also said that he didn't think he could get a taxi to come out but he would call.

A cab finally did come and took us to the Miami International Airport. Right in the middle of the baggage conveyor there was carpeting. We slept on the carpeting. Every hour a loud buzzer would sound and a crowd of people would get their luggage off the conveyor. I ignored it. I ignored everything from that honeymoon all the way through to the divorce.

Edit Draft Blue

7/17/07 3 am (God woke me up with this at both 1 a.m. and 3 a.m., with me hearing myself singing it.)

Blue Whale

Like a beached whale   (2nd time through change beached to blue)
I rode into shore
On the wave of your love
I crashed on the floor

I need the tide to turn
To take me back to sea
Into the depths
Where I was meant to be

I need to swim the deep
The deep waters where
I can swim so free
And breathe the salty air

Where I can dive the deep
Where no man can see
Then shoot to the top
Where I can be free

(chorus)

Spirit of the deep
And crisp salty air
Where I'm free to release
What I was called to share
When I'm free to be
What I was born to be

Edit Draft Daniel

7/17/07 noon (I'm back at the Lodge from Bertie's Tuesday Bible Study. I was writing this as she was speaking on the book of Daniel.)

(Book of Daniel)
(I just noticed that Jaziel rhymes with Daniel)
(Bertie said that an apocalypse is the secret purpose of God.)

Daniel

A vision of the future   (ours)
Interpret it or die

Pray for ever and ever
He has the power
Wisdom to the wise
Knowledge to the scholar

Daniel in the lion's den
He was in his eighties!
Angelic visitations
Demons sent from Hades

God's last attempt to pull
His beloved back
By letting them be captive
Kidnapped, taken, in lack   (us in the marriages we were in)

Handsome and intelligent
Courageous, healthy, strong
God honoring and seeking
Wisdom, knowledge of God   (all about you)

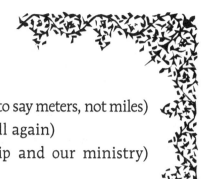

Babylon, shaped like a square	(tradition)
Fourteen long miles	(this is supposed to say meters, not miles)
A 300 foot tall wall with	(there's that wall again)
Footings deep at thirty-three feet	(our relationship and our ministry)
	(33=Jesus age)

So fortified	(our love: living, growing, beautiful, God made)
No one could ever harm	(not able to be torn down by anyone)
The Hanging Gardens	
Of Babylon	

Darius took over the kingdom	
At the age of sixty-two	
And Daniel proved more capable	
At the age of eighty, too.	(you just keep getting better)

(6:21)	
Shut the mouth of the lion, Lord!!	(lion=Rich)
Seeking to devour	
Roll away the stone, Lord	(his coldness and hardness of heart)
And find the lion cowered	(at the power of God)

(chapter 9, 10: 12-14)

The coming of the Messiah	(soon)
The time of entrance here	
Angelic beings speaking	
Demonic forces in fear	

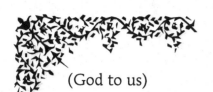

(God to us)

As you go your ways
You will rest at the
End of your days
Again you, you will rise
In the inheritance
That is in, in His eyes
In God's sovereign power
We can recognize
When things are impossible
And life is unfair
What will we see?
A miracle comes
When we are in need
Prayer and fasting
Breaks the holds
Where darkness
Seems to be   (What is your prayer?)

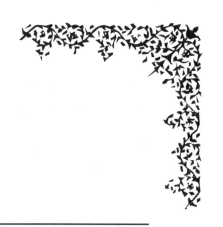

Chapter 13

From: AlexaColjen@msn.com
To: JazBachman@msn.com
Subject: Holy Spirit 1977
4/18/2007 01300:0000
Attachment 1977

1977

When I had received the baptism of the Holy Spirit, I wasn't in a perfect marriage. There wasn't any sin involved that anybody could really point out. However, lack of good marriage, or lack of anything else that is good, is totally against the Bible.

Anyway, I was invited to a Full Gospel Businessmen's Banquet, which was held in a swanky hotel banquet room. It was for women, too. At the time, I was working at the local Christian radio station as an advertising account executive, so I was qualified to attend.

My radio station boss was a minister/psychologist. Everything I told him freaked him out. When I told him I wasn't living in sin, he said, "Really?" as if he didn't believe me or something. Then he said, "Were you a cheerleader in high school?" I don't know what he had meant by that, other than maybe that I was good at encouraging people to buy advertising or cheering them on to do whatever. Everybody but Rich, that was.

So, there I was at Full Gospel and there was a served dinner and a speaker. I don't remember what the speaker said or what the message was, except for two of his sentences. At the end of his speech, he said, "Anybody who wants to be saved, come to the front."

I was already saved so I didn't go up. Then he said, "Anybody who wants to be baptized in the Holy Spirit, come up."

Well, I didn't know what that meant, but as far as I knew I wasn't baptized in it, so I went up.

My friend, Signey Clark, a businesswoman who had invited me, as well as two other normal looking business people took me into a maintenance closet. I wondered if this kind of baptism had anything to do with mops and buckets. They said to just thank God for being God and for everything. I did that. Then they put their hands on my head and prayed for me to receive the baptism.

WOW! My legs felt like somebody plugged me into a 220 electric outlet! They said to keep thanking God and when I run out of words just use whatever words come out of my mouth and if I get tired, just kneel down. I immediately knelt because I couldn't stay standing with God touching my legs. What I was saying sounded kind of like baby talk.

"That's good," they said.

It was.

Edit Draft Legs with note at bottom

7/19/07 4am-4:02 am

(I woke myself up singing this out loud. It took two minutes to write it into Drafts, including logging in.)

(It's a boogie woogie rock and it sounds kind of like "Boogie Woogie Choo Choo")

Electric Legs

(God to me)

> We're not goin' to a clambake
> That would be a miss take
> I didn't give you 'lectric legs
> Just so you could stay in one place

Get out there and move it girl
Dance like there's no tomorrow
This is the time of your life
No not a time of sorrow

I said get out there and move it
Move some things around
Get out there and move it
You're gonna shake up that town

Tell it to the preacher
Tell it to the judge
Tell it to this whole earth
That I love them so much

I said I love them
I said I love them so much
That's right girl you heard me
I said I'm still in love

(4:20 am. God woke me and said, "Babe, I promised you'd write the lyrics for Jaz's songs. He already has the music for this one and for most of the others you wrote down. Ask him to find Electric Legs.")

(Do you remember that? When God told me that *you* would write the music for my lyrics, when I didn't even know if you could write music? So, I'm supposed to ask you to find some things now. Hmm. Jaz, would you please and kindly find the boogie woogie music for Electric Legs and most of the others I wrote down?)

(Wow! The God of the Universe is asking you, Jaziel Bachman, to find some music! That's why I gotta stay pure, so I can hear the songs and Him giving you messages! Are you hearing the same thing from Him? You better be, because if you're not it means I'm making this up and I'm not making this up so the other alternative is that I'm coo coo. I guess that could be a possibility, but not too likely. This is too exciting! Better let me know right away because I'm not gonna sleep till I hear that you found the music for this. Then I'm gonna look through and pick out all the ones that God gave me directly out of His mouth. I will keep you posted. No

I'm not gonna wait, I gotta start looking though now. GTG. I'm not going back to bed. What time do you get up?)

To Alexa:

I get up at 8 in the summer. It's 8 am now. When do you sleep?

I've already got a Bo Diddley war chant on Lectric Legs, but zapped up to the end times.

Jazzy be rockin good.

Edit Draft God's Game

7/20/07 8:00 a.m. Oswald: "Dependent on God's Presence", the word "walk" is used to express the character of a person. Gen 17:1 NIV God to Abraham: "Walk with me." Psalm 46 NIV "we will not fear", an understanding of the ever presence of God, and "be still" meaning STOP and listen to the voice of God.

God's Game

What God is telling me this morning
Is that I don't have to be afraid
He is always with me
That's how this game is played

He's gonna tell me what to do
All I have to do is listen
He'll say what move to make
Life and love will glisten

It's not that he ever left me
Or that He didn't care
It's that I wasn't listening hard
I wasn't willing to share

I didn't give my time to Him
He had to wait for me
I didn't listen to what He said
I chose my right for me

I want to be like Abraham
Who walked right next to God
And Samuel and the others
Who heard from God aloud

And I want to be like David
Who praised Him with his songs
And I want to be like Jesus
Who laid his own desires down

(I'm crying now...I am a selfish wretch.)

Edit Draft Ice Road Truckers

Tuesday 7/24/07 midnight (At 10 pm, I watched "The History Channel: Ice Road Truckers". It was about hauling a diamond scrubber and the most experienced was the youngest, named Jay Westgard, so triple the interpretation.)

Ice Road Truckers

Truckers on the ice road
Rollin over slippery ice
Haulin ninety thousand pounds
For DeBeers Diamond Mines

Forty degrees past zero
Accidents, breakdowns, worse
Send some truckers packin
And some leave in a hearse

Rollin over frozen lakes
Across Canadian land
For the thrill of freezin
And takin home three grand

Rollin over frozen lakes
Ice pushed to the limit
Take 'er easy Trucker J
Experience is your ticket

(chorus)

Haul that diamond scrubber
Over roads of ice
Where the road meets rubber
Is a solid lake of ice

Alexa,

I drove trucks over the ice road when we lived in Moosinee. Once I volunteered to drive a load of building materials for a church way up north.

Over and out,

Jazz Man (You were right, Jazz Man was my handle.)

Edit Draft Restoration
7/25/07 Tuesday night 1 a.m.
Isiah 64:6, Amos 9:11-15 NIV

Restoration

And what does the Lord say to you?
That he gives and takes away?
According to our righteousness
Which is as filthy faded clothes?
But the righteousness of Christ

Is living in us, those He chose.
No, not in anything we do or say
Not in how we act or live or pray
But only in Him inside of us
You can't get closer than that
And all we have to do is ask

On that day He will raise our fallen tent
The seasons of harvest will run in step
With new wine flowing from the hills
We will rebuild the ruined villages
And live in the fortified towns
We will drink the wine of our vineyard
And eat from the garden we found
We will live on our own land
Always on our own ground
On the land that God has given us
In the Word from His own mouth

Edit Draft Fire, Smoke and Mirrors

7/27/07 5 am (God woke me with this. Words and vision. The third stanza is especially vivid. Word for word out of God's mouth. There's a forest fire and you will be hauling a helicopter out to spray it. You're driving away and watching it in the side view mirror. Be careful. There's also someone out there, a man, that needs to hear the Word. You're going to sing it for him and he'll be saved.)

(And don't worry, when you need it, there's plenty of communication out there. You have to leave from an FBO for the copters. There's internet and everything else. For goodnight's sake, I've even got a Ham Radio operation right here. Dale is all registered to the max. He talks to people in China with a microphone. He also does dispatch for the Abraham Lake Fire Department. That's only if you need it. I can hear you without any electronic stuff.)

(Go with blessings. I'll be praying for you every waking moment and that's a lot because I'm not doing much sleeping.)

Proverbs 2:8 NIV He guards the course of the just and protects the way of his faithful ones.

(rock, classical guitar, in a raspy alto voice)

Fire Smoke and Mirrors

I hear your need
Need to be alone
To hear His voice
Not mine on the phone

Take your guitar
And words for Scarred
There's someone there
That needs the Lord

I see fire and smoke   (our love)
In your side view mirror   (a reflection of God's love)
You're leaving the forest   (confusion)
Watching it clear   (burning up the confusion)

Communication   (God and I are both saying this verse to you
Won't be broken   as well as you saying it to me)
You're in my heart
With words unspoken

(chorus)

I'm alone
I'm not alone
I'm alone
I'm not alone

180

Edit Draft Singing

8/2/07 2:40 am (I started taking singing lessons a few months ago so that I could sing what I'm hearing into my phone in case I'm out walking when I get a song. Maybe I can figure out how to send you a recording when I get good enough at singing and recording.)

(country)

Singing Lessons

You have to open your mouth
Really big to get the right sound
But you have to be relaxed
And make your mouth real round

I can open my mouth
That's been my problem all along
I didn't open my mouth
I let somebody trounce me Bong!

Why did I let him get away with being mean
Why didn't I say I won't put up with that
The other time when he said he was leaving
You big old big green mean machine

Good riddance and don't go too slow
Hurry up I don't have all day
Don't let the screen door hit you
Or trip over the dog on your way

I didn't want to be like one of those women
That's all, all, all alone
Sitting all by herself
No one on the phone
They push away the only man they have
Maybe for a chance for a better one

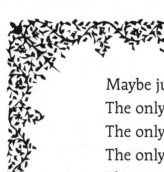

Maybe just because that's the only salve
The only choice
The only method
The only thing
They just make their mouth round and sing

Edit Draft Charity
8/2/07 2:48 a.m.

Charity Bash

I don't particularly feel like I'm in the Spirit
Or the Spirit is particularly in me
I prayed that it would be
But it seems to have left for the night

Probably cause my heart isn't right
Oh yeah that's what it's about
You're not supposed to get online
And let your feelings out

Oh no you're not supposed to do that
No, you're supposed to be real good
You're supposed to think about helping the poor
Widows and orphans and those on the floor

Be like Mother Teresa
And Princess Di
Just one charity bash after another
Then go home and cry

From: AlexaColjen@msn.com
To: ssolack@msn.com
8/5/2007 00300:00

Hi Sandy,

I wrote a song, and revised it to include your name. I saw you and Darryl at church this morning but I had to leave early.

Thanks so much for cleaning some of the houses that I have on the market. I need to give you a check from the "missing ashes" cleaning job you did! I hope they don't notice that there's no ashes in that urn anymore. How were you supposed to know that those weren't cigarette ashes? It's not like they had that urn labeled or something.

Don't forget to mark the next Women's Retreat on your calendar, Sept. 14 & 15, and help me spread the word, OK? Bertrande Solidino, Carol Pickax and I hope Signey Clark will be speaking and the topic is going to be "God'sTiming". Music will be Delores and the Gals and some soloists.

You did a great job last year with check-in and kitchen. Do you want to volunteer your help again this year? No charge again this year for any of the women who attend.

Love to you,
Alexa

8/5/07 Revision (re-vision)

Sandra Dee

Hey y'all Sandra Dee,
Missed you on Sunday. (pronounced Sundy)
Did you have company?
It's 3 am, I can't sleep!

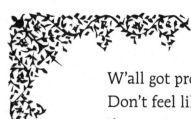

W'all got problems, Sandy
Don't feel like y'all alone
I'm praying for y'all right now
Just like on the phone.

(chorus)

Prayin God gives ya' peace.
Not comin' from any man.
Sure God loves you and me.
He's got us in His plan.

Just be happy, Sandra Dee
You ever see how happy
Some ol' wives can be
You ever see how happy

Stopped tryin' to get their
Husband's love, got the Lord
You ever see how happy
You ever see how happy

Just the Lord and their babies
Got grandkids, you're lucky.
Missed you on Sunday. (Sundy)
Did you have company?

(repeat chorus)

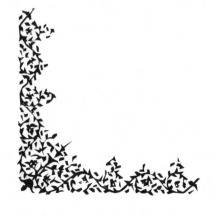

Edit Draft Back to Reality

8/5/07 (Rich's Texas relatives, Windy & Victoria, are visiting me and staying at the Lodge.)

(country rock)

Back to Reality

Ya gotta fill up them days
So ya don't think about it
Sooner or later, ya got it
Ya gotta come back to reality

(chorus)

I'm gonna keep my mind off it
Not gonna think about it
Till you come back to me
Ya gotta come back to reality

Ya gotta keep your mind off it
Ya gotta make some profit
Sooner or later ya got it
Ya gotta come back to reality

(chorus)

I'm gonna keep my mind off it
Not gonna think about it
Till you come back to me
Ya gotta come back to reality

Edit Draft Five

8/6/07 10:30 am (I'm back from a two hour walk. God told me again I'm gonna live to be 105 years old. I met Tina Memery's grandma last month who is 105. She takes care of herself and said she thinks maybe she is "getting to the age" when she should start looking for a nursing home! She lives in Florida in a trailer park. She said to come visit and gave me her address. She said I remind her of the stewardess on the plane she took to New York. She said that when I come to visit she wants to make me a sandwich for lunch!)

Five Years

God says
I'm gonna live to be
A hundred and five
So I'm glad I'm alive
I'm almost half-way there

I better take care
And eat right and sleep
And exercise and keep
My mind fit and all

And when the Death
Angel comes to call
I'll be glad I was alive
When I'm a hundred and five

I gotta write as many songs
As Fannie Crosby
Six thousand and three
Maybe more for me

That's gonna take a while
Maybe five years from now
That's not so long
Not for that many songs

Edit Draft Emma and others

8/16 6am Thursday (Obituary, *Daily News*, Tues, Aug 14, 2007, "Oldest person dies at 114")

Emma Tillman

It's common to live to one o five
Brooke Astor herself just died
She gave away nearly 200 mil
And died on Monday, she wasn't ill

She was mostly concerned
With putting the late husband's estate
To the use of others
And that made her great

She won the civilian honor in '98
The Presidential Medal of Freedom
The nation's highest civilian award
Given to a woman from New York

But Astor didn't even make the lead
She was usurped by Yone Minagawa
On Monday she passed away
The same as Astor, the very same day

According to the Guinness book
The world's oldest person,
Yone was born in 1893
Died the same day as Ms. Society

Emma Faust Tillman died earlier this year
She lived to be a hundred fourteen, too
In the United States, with a smile on her face
She was one of God's chosen, one like you

187

Edit Draft Glorifies

8/8/07 9 am and noon

Dear Drafts,

(No realty appointments this week. No reality appointments this week. I gave myself the week off. Yeah! I can do whatever I like. I'm going to write this song and then see what happens next.)

Here's the Magnificat/Glorifies sounds like Bach & Meatloaf mixed.

8/8/07 9am Luke 1:46-55 NIV 8/9/07 noon (Latin) (Bach in D)

Glorifies Magnificat

The magnificent God lives in me	Magnificat anima mea
Marvelous, joyful and free	Et exulsivit spiritus meus
He ponders the state of my flesh	Quia repexit humilitatum
All generations will call me blessed	Omnes generationes

Powerful God has done miracles for me	Quia fecit mihi magna
Holy is His wonderful way, Holy, Holy, Holy	
His mercy is given to we who fear	Et misericordia
From generations of yesteryear	

He has done miracles of power and grace	Fecit potentiam
Scattering the arrogant from place to place	
He has laid kings and princes on the ground	Deposuit potentes
While raising the lowly to wear a crown	

He has given the choicest foods to me	Esurentis implevit bonis
But sends the rich from the table, empty	Sicut locutus est
He upholds Israel, His faithful slave	Susepit Israel
With mercy filling the promise He gave	
Gloria Patri	

(Latin is a language that no one speaks. I took four years of it at our high school and then two years at University so I translated some of Glorifies. Make what you want of it. I don't know what the music sounded like when anybody actually spoke Latin. I hear something like the modern day "Tommy", the musical by The Who.)

Edit Draft Zebulun & Nephtali
8/22/07 9 am Matt 4:15 & 16 NIV

Zebulun and Nephtali

Giants and soldiers of fear
All the way to the sea
Along the Jordan, they will hear
All the way to Galilee

People living in sin so dark
Will see a marvelous light
Like the morning sun to those
Living under a shadow of night

Music is their shepherd
They'll hear His love in your voice
And when they hear of His love
They will make their choice

They will make their choice

And when they hear of His love
They will make their choice

Edit Draft Sweetness

9/14/07 4:30 a.m. Written in the middle of the Fall Christian Women's Retreat at Coljens Lodge. I had been up front with the musicians and singers, playing my tambourine and singing my heart out. I got up in the middle of the night because I heard "Sweetness". I don't think anybody else heard it because there were about fifty women sleeping in the Lodge and nobody got up. I looked around and I was the only one who was up.

Sweetness of Your Spirit

(chorus)

> The sweetness of your spirit
> When voices praised your name
> Was how I loved to hear it
> When your Spirit came

> When your Spirit hears our voices
> Lifted up in song
> When your Spirit hears the music
> Of our singing all day long

> That's when you come to join us
> In spirit and in truth
> That's when we feel your sweetness
> And when your love is loosed

(chorus)

> The sweetness of your Spirit
> When voices praised your name
> Was how I loved to hear it
> When your Spirit came

9/25/07 9 a.m.

Dear Pink,

No word from Jaz here ... and Rich going on and on to our kids about how he is so glad he divorced me. Like that's news, he threatened divorce almost every day. Promises, promises. No reason. At least he finally followed through on something. He should go on some kind of a pill.

I had dinner last night with Lucy Lou Kramer, Pastor's secretary. She's been on anti-depressants for about four years, and sleeping pills. She said she has to take all kinds of pills; her church job and her boss stress her out. We laughed our heads off about that.

Edit Draft What God is telling me

10/9/07 4am

(What God is telling me:)

Be good. Don't make me jealous. Be careful what you say.

I care about you more than the universe. That will disappear, but you will still be with me in heaven. Don't worry. I will give you plenty to laugh about. Don't worry about what you will eat or where you will lay your head. Look how I have provided for you from the day you were conceived.

(Thank you, Lord)

About J: Yes, I am showing you what it is like to be loved. I am letting you enjoy that. I don't want you to be lacking. The love you feel is from me. I put that love in his heart.

I hoped to provide even more love for you through the other husband, but he wouldn't let me. If he would have loved you, I would not have allowed the divorce. When the opportunity presents itself, you can go to J. Don't look back. Don't turn into a pillar of salt, someone who is caught up in their own worth. All that you are is because I have allowed you to live and given you all that you need.

You will always have ME. I love you more than anything.

It's ok to cry. I'm sad with you. I'm sorry that you made the wrong choices.

That won't last. In the morning you will see my smile. I will give you what you need to go through every day … with power. You have my Holy Spirit with you. Don't forget. The angels are with you.

Trust me. I won't let you down. You'll never wonder what you are supposed to eat or drink if you go where I take you.

Yes, you can share this with Jaz. You can share my love for you with whomever you choose if they want to hear.

(Lord, I want to tell everyone what you are doing for me and how you love me!)
I love you, too, Babe.
(Thank you Lord!!)
(Lord, what about J's former wife?)
You worry too much. Trust me.
(And my kids?)
Yes.
(The music?)
Yes. Everything I do is successful.
(Will you write me a song now?)

     Put your trust in me
     I'll show you where to be
     I'll tell you where and when
     I'll be with you and then

     Then together we will rise
     Our praises fill the skies
     Our songs are like the birds
     Like nothing ever heard

     You are my precious love
     The apple of my eye
     I formed you with my hands
     And made you by and by

Come with me
Be my bride
Be my love
With joy inside

(I love that! What do you call that, Lord?)
Joy Inside

Edit Draft Basking

10/10/07 (midnight) 12:05 am

Basking

People are like open sores
Waiting to be healed
Why are they so unhappy
This world just isn't real

I don't live here anymore
I live in heaven's realm
Where God and I are face to face
And there is no one else

My Lord and I enjoying
Enjoying each other's presence
He's always there whenever I wish
Never thinking me a pestilence

He shares my thoughts, my dreams
My sorrow, fear and joy
He knows my every emotion
I am not His toy

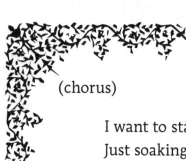

(chorus)

> I want to stay here forever
> Just soaking up your love
> And basking in the sunshine
> Of your glowing from above

Edit Draft Intuity

10/10/07 12:40 am (God, I love this one! These might be some of the best words I ever heard!)

Intuity

> Have you ever seen a spider
> Crawl up a garden wall
> And build a web so pretty
> That it could catch us all
>
> It glistens in the sunlight
> And wavers in the wind
> And has the strength of talons
> Though it is oh so thin
>
> Yet fragile as a butterfly
> A feather or a moth
> A delicate sanctuary
> Of beauty when betrothed
>
> And every poet lurking
> Behind its metaphor
> Sees only traps and lies
> Deceit and sin's disguise

Can't they see the beauty
Of God's magnificent design
And way of His provision
Purpose, form and line

A work of art
A thing of beauty
God's creative
High intuity

Chapter 14

Edit Draft Jealousy

10/11/07 5 am

1 Samuel. When Saul was prophesying, out of jealousy, he threw a spear at David.

Jealousy: the fear that someone else may get or already have what you desire.

(I just keep writing down what I hear, mostly in the middle of the night. I didn't realize, before, how cute the Pez dispensers are. I wonder if that design idea came to somebody in the middle of the night. I wish I could think of something that clever.)

Jealousy

Jealousy is a terrible thing
It racks our minds
So we can't sing
It tracks the motions
Of slaves and kings
And rules their hearts
When they want something

Psalm twenty-three
The Lord is my shepherd
I shall not want.

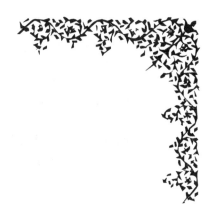

Those whose trust is in the Lord
Have all that God himself can afford
Power, wealth and the love of people
Warmth and joy beneath a steeple
Creation's glory in a rushing wind
Forgiveness even when they've sinned

Psalm one hundred and three
All that I have and all that I own
I owe to God and him alone
Forgiveness, healing and redemption
Love, mercy and youthful retention
He has it all and freely gives
Only because of him, I live

Bless God O my soul
Let not a jealous thought enter in
Keep me humbly away from sin
Watch me from your heavenly throne
Make my heart your happy home
Angels! Bless the God of heaven
Armies at his beck and call
Do what he says! Do it all!
Bless Him, all that he has made
Bless Him, in all that you say
May I bless you Lord every day
May I bless you Lord in every way

(Finished 5:30 am)

Jaz,

It is so strange. I go to bed, and while I'm sleeping, God must put all this stuff in my head. Then I wake up and out it pours. I didn't look up anything for the above lyric, "Jealousy". It was just there. If I try, on my own, to think up a song or

write something, there's nothing there. Also, I can't remember anything I've ever written down. Maybe one line, here and there, but that's about it.

Remember I had told you that I'm taking voice lessons so that I could sing what I'm hearing and record it on my phone? Yesterday, Shelly, my voice teacher, said, "God has something for you to do. He's using you as His vessel."

I lost weight since my divorce and I am now like a thinner, higher pitched, vessel. Ha ha! Shelly made me sing soprano. I usually sang alto in church before the divorce. No, I was not fat before the divorce! I maintained my schoolgirl figure. She said, "In a short time, you're going to be incredible!" She was very excited. She usually doesn't get too excited about much. Shelly didn't want me to leave.

Edit Draft Balloon

10/11/07 1 pm (I was driving back from a church meeting with the Equipping Pastor. He wanted to consult with me about Women's Ministries. After that, I had the pleasure of personal "counseling" from Lucy Lou Who, the church secretary. She's a caring soul.)

Balloon

You are like a magnificent (yes, you)
Rainbowed, silk balloon
Rising with passion's flames
I can ride on the top, crossed legs
Or in the basket surveying the plains

Carried by the gentle breeze
Or rushing high above the trees
I'm content here in the sky (I'm just happy, that's all)
With the clouds as they roll by
In the sunshine, you and I

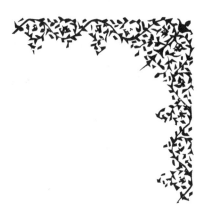

Edit Draft Fragile

10/11/07 11:30 pm

Fragile

I am a fragile reed
Leaning upon a tree
A wisp of a will
Once strong until
Faced with what will be

You will have to come for me
And place me in your hand
And carry me to the island
Where once again I'll stand

And set me on a solid rock
Of love that never shifts
Your promised refrain
May I hear it remains
Unchanging as I drift

Dear Pink,

10/12/07 8 am

Psalm 40:17 The Message Bible//Remix "And me? I'm a mess. I'm nothing and have nothing: make something of me. You can do it; you've got what it takes--but God, don't put it off."

God to me: I love you. Do you see how much Jaz loves you? (Yes.) I love you with a love much greater even than that. Do you think that I would ever leave you? (No.) Or let you be blown away by the winds of circumstance? (No.) Be happy and sing. Trust me, I won't give you more than you can handle. I'm making you stronger than you have ever been before. I want everyone to see my strength in you. (God, I will give you the credit.)

Edit Draft Hand

10/12/07 8:30am God just pointed this passage out, I didn't concordance it or anything, just when I wanted to quit accepting the Platinum Corp foreclosure avoidance assignments to me as a Realtor. Now there are more houses with For Sale signs in our town than there are without them.

Romans 15:1-6 The Message//REMIX "Those of us who are strong and able in the faith need to step in and lend a hand to those who falter, and not just do what is most convenient for us. Strength is for service, not status. Each one of us needs to look after the good of the people around us, asking ourselves, 'How can I help?'

Hand of Provision

He pulled me up
With his strong arm
To where the land
Is safe and warm

Out of the pit
Of pity and grief
To where his love
Was of relief

I love him more
Than words can tell
More than the stars
Or realms of hell

I'll follow Him
Where he may go
To heaven's gate
Or the dark below

And bring the others
On this great land
Right to our Lord
Show them His hand

Edit Draft 3 am Joke

10/16/07 3am God tells me jokes. I don't tell people this because then they'll think I'm crazy. Anyway, I'm giving Him the credit.

God: What is the difference between a cooler full of ice and a linebacker?
Me: I don't know.
God: You can pack more beer into the linebacker.

Me: God, can I go back to sleep now?
God: You can change it to Gatorade if you're telling it to kids.
Me: I am so tired.
God: OK

Chapter 15

10/18/07 Business Gray Notebook

Some 5 am thoughts:

I should leave here and go to Canada
Maybe I should bring a Cabela's blow-up mattress so we can go wherever we want
I won't be bringing my big trophy but I should bring my black belt
Figure out what pan(s) to bring
Bring grandparent's silver so it doesn't disappear
Take pix of my artwork, especially the cardinals
Take pix of karate trophies, especially the big ones
Don't forget some clarinet reeds & music
Figure out what notebooks to bring and which ones to burn
Bring lighthouse decorations that I have been stockpiling

9 am thoughts:

bring birth certificate
other important papers & account codes
winter coat
bathing suit
maybe I won't bring anything ... just my toothbrush
It's raining here. I love rain. The sky and the lake are both gray. It's beautiful. God is so good to me to let me look at this and have the attention of Jaz at the same time.

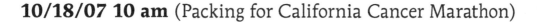

10/18/07 10 am (Packing for California Cancer Marathon)

Misty day. Oswald Chambers, "The Key to the Missionary's Devotion", 3 John 1:7 " ... they went forth for His name's sake, without any help from the pagans."

Romans 5:5 "the love of God has been poured out in our hearts by the Holy Spirit ... That love comes in contact with everyone I meet. I remain faithful to his name even though the common sense view of my life may seemingly deny that, and may appear that he has no more power than the morning mist ... The key to the missionary's devotion is that he is attached to nothing and to no one except our Lord himself."

Morning Mist/H2O

When the cares of this world
Fade into the morning mist
And my concerns are reduced
To an unimportant list

Then the love of Jesus
Is all that I can touch
And I am overwhelmed
That He could love so much

And I am filled to overflowing
With the love He has for me
That spills onto the feet
Of those he brings to me

And though I am a vapor
With no power of my own
He waters the fields with
His own chemistry, H 2 O

Pink Notebook

10/22/07 Sunday night in San Francisco. 2 am Pacific Standard Time (5am EST, my time)

(hip hop)

Fresh Love

Uh oh!
I think I'm in love
I think I fell in deep
Into a bottomless well so sweet

Oh oh!
I don't wanna climb out
Just leave me alone in here
No darkness, no pain, no fear

Oh! Oh!
Send down a bucket
I'll give you a taste
It's fresh and cool and clear

Oh! Oh!
Fresh love so cool and clear
Fresh love so cool and clear
Fresh love so cool and clear

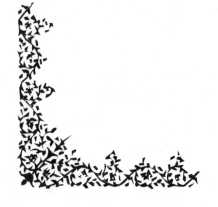

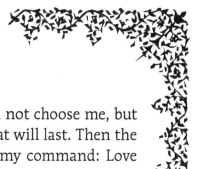

Edit Draft Chosen Fruit

10/25/07 10:30 am "I chose you" John 15:16, 17 "You did not choose me, but I chose you and appointed you to go and bear fruit---fruit that will last. Then the Father will give you whatever you ask in my name. This is my command: Love each other."

Chosen Fruit

It wasn't me who chose you God
But in wisdom you chose me
To do your will and love you still
No matter what the cost may be

And when I feel as fragile
As a falling golden leaf
I look to the sky and find that I
Am strong within your keep

I am nothing without you Lord
I have no wish or will
Keep me close, don't let me boast
Of anything, nothing, nil

And when your fruit is ripened
That's when you'll hear my prayer
That all will see your goodness
In the love that you have shared

(chorus)

Hold me in your hand Lord
Like a ripe and luscious fruit
May I satisfy your every cry
As I only speak the truth

Edit Draft Chosen Fruit Reply

I loved that one and I think that many others will also.

Jaz

Edit Draft Glitzy Girl

10/25/07 Thurs night 1 a.m. and 4 a.m. (If I don't get up the first time, God just wakes me up with the same song later. He's patient like that.)

(I hear you, Jaz, playing a super-bad rockin' guitar riff.)
(hard rock)

Glitzy Girl

Hey Glitzy Girl (Bam)
Rock out your heart
Rock out your soul

Hey Glitzy Girl (Bam)
Rock out your heart
Make yourself whole

(Bam, Bam Bam Bam
Bam, Bam Bam Ba bam
Bam Bam Bam Bam)
Rock it out hard (Bam)
Rock it out hard (Bam)
Rock it out hard (Bam)
Hey Glitzy Girl (Bam)
(repeat all over and over and over)

Edit Draft No Idea

10/26/07 7am

(I dreamt our wedding. We looked like we do now.)

Jesus married us. He had a looong train, light brown looong hair, and a looong beard. I had on a cream gown with little clear beads on the front and you had on a black tux. Do you own one?

Immediately after, you were sitting down and there were two empty music stands by you and a table with our half eaten wedding cake. We didn't know who ate it

I had a huge white envelope with wedding pictures but they weren't photographs. They were drawings, some color pencil and some sepia, already matted and shrink wrapped. The color drawings were modernistic, just shapes and lines … Primary colored small geometric shapes connected by black curved lines. The sepia one was of us and Jesus at the altar. I brought them over to your left side and asked if you wanted to see the pictures. You said yes.

I said, "They give you drawings. If I would have known the Pastor was going to have a long train, I would have had one too. Where did you find him?"

You said, "He's kind of a hippie."

My dad came up to us (he was about the age when we were in HS) and sat down across from you. He said he couldn't see the pictures on that side of you, so I brought them to your right side. (Dad always used his left eye more.) Dad had two little smudges of white cake frosting on his face. When he saw the drawing of Jesus marrying us, he fell off the chair. Then he got back up and said, "I've never seen pictures like that before."

I said, "Dad, let me get the frosting off your face." Then I looked for a clean napkin in front of you, but they all had frosting all over them.

I think I can interpret most of this dream but I'm not sure about the frosting all over all the napkins. The primary colored little shapes are the kids we already had. Sepia drawings represent something that existed in the past, in this case, our emotional connection. The cake represents our beautiful union but it was half eaten up by my Dad, who didn't want me to get married to you at a young age and

he had a close and good relationship with me that he enjoyed instead of me taking off with you. Jesus is a hippie because hippies are all about freedom and love. Left is liberal, right is conservative. The long train is the Holy Spirit

I'm sure you could extend the interpretation, extending it to the prophetic, for us and Biblically. I guess we won't have to decide what to wear.

Edit Draft Jesus with Looong Train Reply

I'm full of wonder and laughter!

Jaz

Edit Draft Catch

10/28/07 Sunday morning 7 am (easy running arpeggios in a major key)

Catch and Release

Sparkling sun on a glittering stream
Cold clear water running free
Speckled trout up to our knees
And with your smile God is pleased

Falling leaves of silver of gold
Drop to the water where life is bold
And float on the current running fresh
To the bank where sand and pebbles mesh

Look to the clear blue brilliant sky
Where God has waved his hand on high
And spread the scene with holy peace
And given his Spirit full release

(chorus)

> Catch His Spirit and release
> With your smile God is pleased
> With your hands in the running stream
> Catch His Spirit and release

Lexa you see such beauty ...

Edit Draft Holy Bliss

10/28/07 7:30 am Sunday morning

(While looking at a label on Cashmere Mist lotion: "Indulge yourself while rejuvenating your spirit with the cashmere mist collection. A fragrance that derives its aura of powdery softness from the heliotrope flower. The delicate clusters of purple flowers lend the fragrance of an ethereal, cloud-like caress of cashmere.")

Holy Bliss

> Standing in an open field of flowers
> With the morning cashmere mist
> A sweet caress from God's soft hand
> That says I have been kissed
>
> He's graced me with his fragrance
> A powdery exotic mist
> An aura of delightment
> In a cloud of holy bliss

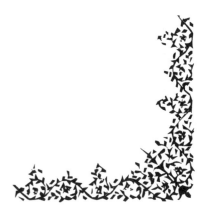

Edit Draft Ministry

10/31/07 8am Matt 6:33 "Seek first the kingdom of God and his righteousness and all these things will be added unto you" Matt 7:7 "Ask and it will be given to you; seek and you will find; and to him who knocks, the door will be opened."

Pastor Anderson decided not to have the planned missionary meeting at my Lodge. Probably because when he asked me, after the divorce, how I am getting along, I said, "Don't ask."

I have another meeting this morning to advise Women's Ministries regarding a new idea that Pastor Anderson wants to implement. Pastor Anderson informed me that the church still wants to have their own Women's Retreat in the spring but not at Coljens Lodge. So, he asked if I would cancel any Christian Women's Spring Retreat at Coljens so that it didn't compete with his plans. I didn't tell him that that would be wonderful for me because I won't be here in the spring to host a retreat, a picnic, a birthday party, a session on underwater basket weaving or anything else.

God is taking away my ministry here but moving me to a different one.

I just said, "Oh, that would be fine."

Why don't people say what they mean? How about, "We don't want someone who we now know is divorced representing the church of Holier Than Thou."

I would respond, "No problem, I will be attending the Church of Saint Mattress of Asleepi."

I feel guilty about not telling them that I am leaving. I feel guilty for breathing. I am totally nut worthy. I mean not worthy. Nut is probably right.

(conversation between God and me)
(style: comedic opera)
(full orchestra)

Ministry

(Me to God, in a loud operatic soprano voice with trilling r's)

How can you use me when I represent a life of selfish sin
I am so unworthy, an empty vessel made of skin
You've given me fullness in ministry
Hundreds praise your name
And call my home a refuge
Now nothing remains the same

(God to me in a gentle bass voice)

I'm moving you to where you can be really used
You think you've walked before
I'm giving you beautiful new walking shoes
Prepare to go out the door

I have a ministry for you that supplants the past
A love that will support you
When your faith seems not to last
I'm bringing you to fullness and everlasting joy
Don't discount the miracles that have brought you to this plan

(music stops)

(acapella Me to God)

How can this be
How can you use someone like me
I can't measure up to what you want me to be

(music starts again)

(God to Me)

211

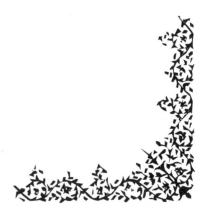

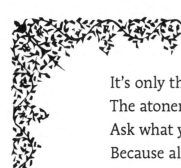

It's only through Christ
The atonement for your sins
Ask what you will and I'll place it within
Because all that you want is to be close to me
I'll grant you your wish, your desire to be free

And after a time, the ministry of mine
Will be not what you've done in the past
But all things are made new
As I give them to you
Through love that forever will last

Edit Draft Your Voice

11/1/07 Thursday midnight. Jaz, I feel so at ease with you. At peace. God shows me what He is like by the way that you communicate with me. God speaks for you. You can go to sleep peacefully knowing that I love you. The confidence in your voice, which I have only heard once this year in the "real" world, is so reassuring. This song is about God but it is about you as well.

(like a Brahm's lullaby)

Your Voice

Peace, rest and comfort
Like a feather pillow for my head
That's how I am with you Lord
When by you I am led.

I want to be with you Lord
Every minute of every day
And hold me while I sleep Lord
Be with me while I pray

Your way is easy Lord
A smooth and gentle ride
That brings me into fullness
When I am by your side

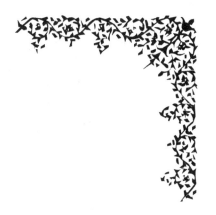

And I know that you want me
And I want to hear your voice
It lets me know that all is well
And that I have made your choice

(chorus)

Your voice is like a blanket
On a cold and starry night
That warms me all around
As I listen with delight.

(Where it says "Lord" I can put "Jaz" in there. I hope God doesn't get too jealous.)

Edit Draft Talking

11/1/07 Thursday night 12:30 am After Women's Ministries meeting. My surroundings have no meaning anymore.

Talking Heads

Is there anyone else in the whole wide world
We're the only ones living here
Everyone else is a talking head
With their mouth flapping in my ear

Don't they know there's nothing else
That matters a bit at all
Than the two of us becoming one
And rising before the fall

And when we come together
It will be like an explosion
Fire seen for miles
From the impact of implosion

What God has joined together
By the force of his own Spirit
Will create a miraculous impact
And all around will hear it

(chorus)
No one else lives on the earth
There's only you and me
What are all those talking heads
You and I are meant to be

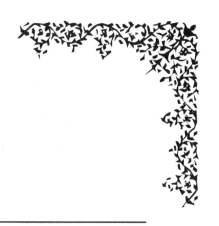

Chapter 16

Edit Draft His Way

11/1/07 Thursday night 12:45 am

Oswald Chambers, "I must be broken from my own understanding of myself ... If I love God, I will do what he says without hesitation. If I hesitate, it is because I love someone I have placed in competition with him, namely myself."

Gal 2:20 NIV "I have been crucified with Christ and I no longer live, but Christ lives in me. The life I live in the body, I live by faith in the Son of God, who loved me and gave himself for me. I do not set aside the grace of God, for if righteousness could be gained through the law, Christ died for nothing!"

Here are my running thoughts: I cannot live to please people. I mean people who think I shouldn't leave home. It is impossible to please everyone, anyway. I can only do what God wants me to do. Although it is humbling to set aside my pride, pride that I have the power to live by the law, when the truth is that Christ is the only one who can live by the law, and He by the Spirit within me. There is contentment beyond words in that. I'm not expressing very well here what I am trying to say. He is gracious and loving and only has what is best for us.

God gives his love to us with no strings attached. You know, it's not like only if we do this or that. He just loves us no matter what and shows us how much. So, some people won't understand, but we understand.

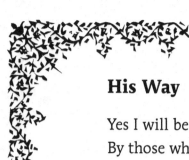

His Way

Yes I will be crucified
By those who don't understand
Who cannot grasp the fullness
Of all that God has planned

Yes I must be broken
From the image of myself
Of someone who can obey the law
Righteous on my own

When I'm willing to be humbled
Enough to live by faith
Not trusting in my fortune
Or the virtue of my face

When I live by His instruction
And trust Him with my soul
That's when He shows His love
His provision and my role

(chorus)

Who I am must be put to death
So that Christ can live in me
Righteousness can only live
When He has his way with me

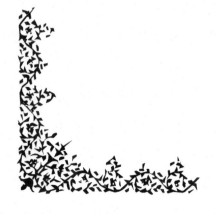

216

Edit Draft Devine Delay

11/4/07 10 pm

Matt 25:14-30 NIV The Parable of the Talents; Matt 25:19 NIV "After a long time ..."
(aria)

Devine Delay

Why is God so gracious to delay
And not push us into prominence
When it is not our day
And wait for us to happen
As we go along the way
So that He can say "Well done
My daughter and my son"

He waited and he waited
He came back from a very long way
He waited before coming back
To settle accounts that day

And why did he wait
What was the purpose there
The man with five and the man with two
Both knew right away what to do

But the master knew
When the time was right
To offer his reward
Blessings from the Lord

Gifts had to be cultivated
They had to blossom and grow
Things that only a master
Only The Master would know

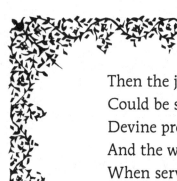

Then the joy of service
Could be shared with the Lord of Hosts
Devine presence of the Father, Son and Holy Ghost
And the welling up inside of the pleasure of the day
When service to the Lord is pleasing in his way
And sharing for a moment, a minute or a day
The happiness that God feels
When we serve him in this way

Edit Draft Can't Teach Desire

11/4/07 11 pm (I am back from the big Nike Run for the Cure Marathon in San Francisco, with thousands upon thousands upon thousands of people. This is a quote from some famous football coach that was repeated by a coach at the Marathon After Party: "You can't coach desire.")

(Also, I heard Jeff Foxworthy on the radio, "You might be a Redneck if ... The experience of your favorite restaurant is enhanced by video tokens." I would have to admit to that.)

(kinda slow country)

Can't Teach Desire

You can't teach desire
It's there or it's not
You can't put the "want to"
Just into any slot

It's not a coin
That you can use
To get the end result
It's not a lesson
In a book
Or a course
That someone taught

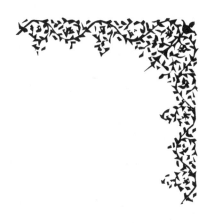

In all your ways acknowledge Him
He will give you the desire
Yes he will give
He will give
He will give you the desire
He will give you the desire
The desire of your heart

(Wow, we have experienced this already for sure. God put the desire there. For each other and to collaborate as well as to serve Him and to help other people.)

(By the way, I finished the race without breaking a sweat and it was a whole lot of fun. All the downtown streets were crowded with racers and spectators at 4 am in the dark with the bright street lights on and bands amped and playing Pump-up Music. Everybody was jumping up and down for a warm up. I've never seen that many excited people in one place.)

Dear Pink,

11/6/07 Almost midnight, after Jaziel had a terrible meeting with some of his church friends who meant well by telling him that a year after his divorce is too soon to consider a relationship with anyone and that since I was divorced ... well, never mind.)

We feel everything deeply, don't we? How blessed I am to know a man that can feel. That has emotions. That doesn't put his emotions aside, put up a wall or wear a mask.

One time I had an assignment in Bible study group to write down all of the emotions that David expressed in the book of Psalms. It was impossible. I filled up a page after reading only a small number of the Psalms. God loved David. I know that God loves Jaz.

Edit Draft Cell

11/6/07 2am (J says he lost his cell and doesn't know where.)

(Did you know that it is almost impossible to cry if your head is tilted up? Something about the physiology of the tear glands. I hope you have a wonderful day today. Look up. Look at the sky. You will feel so happy.)

(Sung in a very twangy country voice)

Cell Phone

> Don't drop your cell phone in the water
> Keep it right just where you oughter
> In its case or your valise
> And if it's lost don't call the police
>
> And best to erase your history
> Back all the way to infinity

(chorus)

> Don't drop your cell phone in the water
> Keep it right just where you oughter
> In its case or your valise
> And please don't call those church police

Edit Draft Psalm 46

11/6/07 almost midnight

God of Daybreak Psalm 46

> God is our hiding place and strength
> He is always there when we are troubled
> If the earth opens under our feet
> And the ocean swells to swallow

220

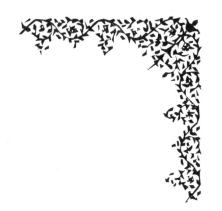

There is a river that streams
Where God, his throne he takes
Watching over us now and ever
God helps us when day breaks

The Lord Almighty is with us
The God of Jacob is our bastion
He makes wars cease
And burns the iron weapons

(joyfully)

(chorus)

God will be highly honored
By the peoples of the lands
The Lord Almighty is with us
The God who lifts his hands

Edit Draft Temple

11/8/07 The land of Oz "We do not know what we should pray for as we ought, but the spirit Himself makes intercession for us ..."

Romans 8:26 The Spirit of God uses the nature of the believer as a temple in which to offer His prayers of intercession.

Romans 8:31 " ... if God is for us, who can be against us? ... "8:37, 38" ... we are more than conquerors through him who loved us ... For I am convinced that neither death nor life, neither angels nor demons, neither the present nor the future, nor any powers, neither height nor depth, nor anything else in all creation, will be able to separate us from the love of God that is in Christ Jesus our Lord."

(powerfully, with lots of lower brass)

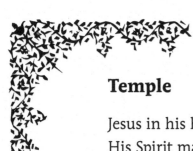

Temple

Jesus in his holy temple
His Spirit makes me whole
And though a mountain shatters
It can't divide my soul

Not a towering inferno
Or depths of widest girth
Not death from hell or any foe
Or life upon this earth

Not time or space or demons
Or any evil power
That roams the land
And takes a stand against me any hour

Will ever separate us
Will ever drive a wedge
Will ever come between us
Or push us to the edge

Edit Draft Already

11/9/07 2:15 pm (It sounds like I'm going to be with you!)

Already There

I'm going to...

Orbit this planet without a rocket
Then veer on an intergalactic flight
Bound for other worlds am I
Into the starry night I'll fly
At the speed of soaring light

My feet have left this planet
Never to return again
What lies ahead
Is in my head
I'm going there fast instead

Powered by love's appointment
A soaring launch
To outer space
A distant place
Where there is no human race

Whooshing past the planets
Past their moons and stars
To God knows where
And I don't care
I am already there

Edit Draft Princess

11/12/07 11:55 pm

Jaz asked his mother, Joan, to make a quilt for us of purple, gold and green, as in "Your Song". I asked her to use tiny triangles.

(regally with lots of brass and sung with a Welsh accent)

Princess Banquet

Maybe I've been starved before
Maybe I've been driven
But now I'm feasting at a table
Of food that I've been given

And tasting every delicious bite
That's set in front of me
Whatever I wish whatever I might
Is what is brought before me

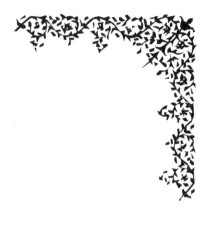

The way you hear what I have written
And turn it into song
And piece the colors that we love
Into a quilt so warm (my voice teacher says not to pronounce "r")

What love is this
What delicious fare
Given to me on a silver plate
Because I am the King's heir

(I'm thinking about maybe hanging the quilt on the wall in your dining room because it will be so beautiful and maybe decorating with a purple and green grapes theme in that room and some gold whatever. What do you think?

Lexie

Maybe we'll use gold paper plates?

Jaz

Edit Draft Screens

11/14/07 1:40 am (I am so sick of all this material stuff. I do not drink beer or wine. I don't know who the chorus is for; you? There are three big screen TV's with HD in the Lodge and a flat screen in all the rooms.)

(most definitely country with a twang)

Big Screens

I've had my fill of big screen TVs
In Technicolor with HD
Talladega Nights
And Ricky Bobby
Give me the simple life

224

I've had my fill of satin sheets
Silver trays and bouginoine beef
Flambéed dessert
Brought to my seat
Give me the simple life

I've had my fill of fancy cars
Rack and pinion steering bars
Convertible
And programmable
Give me the simple life

(chorus)

Give me the life of just a beer
Out at the cabin on a porch at the rear
Lookin at the stars
On any old night
Give me the simple life

Edit Draft Broken Chair

11/20/07 5:30am (warning: don't read this at work unless you have a lot of Kleenex)

(The fact that you fix chairs makes me so happy it brings tears to my eyes: There are a few reasons. It has to do with the fact that you see value in things to the point that you would try to salvage them. Also, I collect wooden chairs. I don't pay much, four dollars is my limit. I have about a hundred of these, because they get used for seating for events at the Lodge. Some of them are very old and fragile and they get used for decorations.)

(I have fixed some of the chairs, myself, with wood glue and clamps.)

(about how God loves us enough to forgive us to restore our soul)

(slowly, with violins)

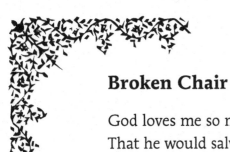

Broken Chair

God loves me so much
That he would salvage me
The wreck that I am
He sees what I could be

He looks at me
And sees a broken chair
And pours out his love
To restore what once was there

What kind of love is this
That sees the worth in me
That cared enough to die
A death upon a tree

(chorus)

A broken life
He can restore
A broken heart
Is there no more

(I am sobbing, God loves me so much and I don't feel like I'm worth his effort)

Edit Draft Unique Process

11/21/07 8:30 am

(God told me to save the tag with the washing instructions from my new white cotton dress because the words on it are a song. "**UNIQUE HAND PROCESS** DUE TO THE UNIQUE PROCESS USED TO CREATE THIS PRODUCT, SLIGHT DIFFERENCES MAY OCCUR, MAKING EACH PIECE AS DISTINCTIVE AS THE INDIVIDUAL WHO WEARS IT. TO HELP MAINTAIN THE CRINKLE EFFECT, SPECIAL WASH CARE IS NEEDED REMOVE DAMP GARMENT FROM WASH, TWIST GARMENT, & TIE TIGHTLY INTO A KNOT, TUMBLE DRY LOW FOR BEST PERFORMANCE"

(oh my! is this interpretation ever tripled! Every line: on the face of it, spiritually and then some)

(style: Nickelback)

Unique Process

He makes us creates us
Into what we are
A unique process
Different for every star (every person)
He makes us each (individual)
Maintains us with care (doesn't turn us into clones of somebody)
He washes us into (with his forgiveness)
Who we should be (holiness)
And puts the beauty there (He makes us like Himself)
While we're still damp (it's an ongoing process, not overnight)
We undergo twisting (His shaping can be painful)
And tying into a knot (marriage)
Tumbling and heat (within marriage)
But when we come out (after all His work on us)
Our performance (triple this)
You cannot doubt (spiritually)

(chorus)

A unique hand process
Only by His hand
We undergo his washing
Now we understand

Edit Draft Ocean of Love

11/22/07 Friday noon Oswald, "Beware of allowing yourself to think that the shallow aspects of life ... eating and drinking, walking and talking ... are not ordained by God ..."

Ocean of Love

Just as surely
As the ocean depths
Have a shallow at the shore
Surely my walk and talk
Have been ordained forevermore

The same God who made the ocean
And the waves upon the beach
Gives the depth of His Spirit
And happiness within reach

Oh the wonder of His order
The turning of the tide
The depths of His forgiveness
And the washing of our pride

(chorus)

Ocean of love
Arrives on the shore
Of a whitewashed beach
Of warmth evermore

Edit Draft Baptized

11/25/07 10:15 pm (I got baptized tonight
at church. I had never done that.)

(It is a COUNTRY song and I pretty much hate Country music.)

Baptized

(chorus)

> I came up out of the water
> Into the brightest light
> And it was a symbol of birth
> Into the world of right

> And Jesus himself was baptized
> And all the early saints
> And all the brand new converts
> And some who really ain't

> I don't know who baptized me
> It felt like it was Christ
> I think it really was Him
> He's the one that paid the price!

(repeat chorus)

> I came up out of the water
> Into the brightest light
> And Jesus himself was waiting
> To catch me on the right

Edit Draft Down

11/26/07 9:30 am (from a prayer, see last night's Blue Notebook entry for the prayer)

Down

Look at me, God
I'm a feather blowing in the wind
What bird did I come from
Where did I begin

Put me to some good use
In a blanket or a pillow
Let me keep someone warm
Don't leave me in a willow

It's cold out here
And I am so afraid
What if I am wrong about
The very plans you've made

What if my destiny
Is not what I had thought
What if all the fear and doubt
Is something you have brought

I can't do this by myself
I need you by my side
I can't be all alone
In this windy world so wide

Keep me in a winter coat
Right next to your heart
Don't let me wonder
If I can fill this part

Edit Draft I'm OK

11/26/07 1:30 pm (After worrying for 6 months about getting rid of a 2nd mortgage on a listed foreclosed property and two offers dropping from it because of that, I am told today by the banker that the 2nd lien holder disappears after the redemption, which is also a real estate term.)

(New offer tendered today, from major competitor's brokerage, and previous offer may renew. I see this as God telling me that he sees everything, he knows my needs, he loves me and he is in control. It is up to God whether this deal closes or not and it is up to God whether J and I end up together, just like everything is actually and eventually up to God.)

I'm OK

God tells me that I'm OK
In His way, in His way
He lets me know with blessings
And the things that people say

And in my heart I know
That He will always be the same
He will always love me
No matter what time or day

He isn't a cruel taskmaster
That says do it my way or else
He isn't a punishing fool
That harms people just for spite
Or punishes their offspring
Because they didn't do it right
He's a merciful God that understands
That sees all the details
Like nobody else can

He tells us what to do
By His Spirit and in His plan
And if we move out of it
We feel His gentle hand

And when we're in His will
It harmonizes with our heart
Our feelings and emotions
Confirm the musical chart

There's a melody of sweetness
And a song within our lungs
And words of adoration are
Spoken with our tongues

Edit Draft Marshmallow Pies

11/26/07 9 pm (It's late. I'm still working at the real estate office, the radio is playing in the background. I'm pretty sure it's the radio. I don't want to think about anything. I just want to have fun.)
(country)

Marshmallow Pies

It's time for everybody to lighten up
Ok does anything really matter
What's all this stuff on the radio
Just a bunch of chitter chatter

The weather in the area
Weird news across the nation
Somebody had a birthday
The traffic on the station

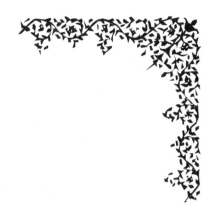

Some music with a heartbeat
Some talk from a local guest
Some tip on how to clean a rug
And what to put in a cedar chest

There's too much information
I hate the internet
I don't care who's dancing with stars
And how much money I could get

Let's just sit by the fire
And toast some marshmallow pies
And think about the heavens
And how God made the skies

Edit Draft Life

11/27/07 4 pm (I don't know for sure what this is about, but I think it's about you working with kids and music)

(easy listening)

Life is Beautiful

Life is beautiful
Life is good
The colors are bright
Everything looks like it should

Bright green trees
With a bright blue sky
Bright white clouds
Go rolling brightly by

Everyone is smiling
Such a happy grin
And children are laughing
With candy on their chin

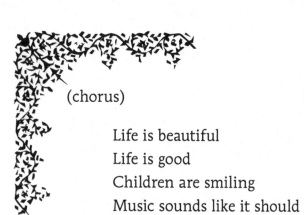

(chorus)

> Life is beautiful
> Life is good
> Children are smiling
> Music sounds like it should

Yes, I teach High School Music, mostly guitar. I also teach music at the University. Did I tell you?

Jaz

Edit Draft God's Address

11/27/07 5pm (I see God in you)

God's Address

> God could live anywhere
> Any country, any part
> But he chose just where he would live
> And he expressly chose your heart
>
> And I know that God does live there
> I know what his address is
> I see how he shines through your face (in my dreams)
> And the kindness of your actions
>
> He found his home there in you
> He chose to live with you
> I see him in the way you look
> And all the things you do

(chorus)

> And that is why I love you
> Because I see my God in you
> And I see He lives right in your heart
> And I want to live there too

Edit Draft Spirit of Joy

11/29/07 8 am (John 16:19-24 ... "In a little while you will see me no more and then after a little while you will see me". God is speaking to me through His word about why it will be difficult now and how it will be joyful now.) (triple this interpretation)

Spirit of Joy

> Although my soul is wrenched
> And pulled from deep within
> By forces from beyond
> That try to drag me into sin   (of not trusting God)
>
> In a little while
> I will see the birth
> Of a precious child (Jesus, our music)
> And my joy will be full
>
> No one can take the joy
> That will be mine alone
> No one will take the One (Jesus, you)
> Who calls my heart his home
>
> In the Spirit we will live
> Trusting God the Father
> Asking in the Son
> For whatever must be done

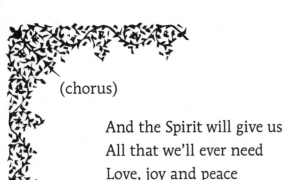

(chorus)

> And the Spirit will give us
> All that we'll ever need
> Love, joy and peace
> A joy that is complete

(This flowed out, with no corrections, as usual, completely written in and by the Spirit of God. Don't give me any credit. I could not repeat one line back to you if I tried. I'm serious and that would be even under the threat of death.)

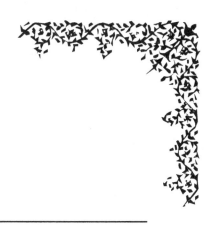

Chapter 17

Edit Draft God, I Missed You

11/29/07 1:15 pm (I exceeded my overdraft protection, I made a deposit and asked for one charge to be removed, then I prayed that they would remove two and they did without me asking for the second one ... Also, I am being given back a listing that shouldn't have been revoked by GMAC REO, relocation division of government real estate department.)

(punk rock)

God, I Missed You

God, I missed you so much
Thank you for talking to me again
Thank you for loving me
And for being my best friend

Where were you God
Did you go on vacation
Did you take a nap
Were you doing something more important
Than listening to all my sap?

Oh you were there all the time?
I just didn't listen to you?
You hear all the things I say
And see all the things I do?

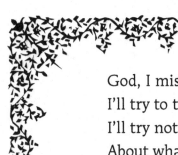

God, I missed you so much
I'll try to trust you more
I'll try not to get all worried
About what you have in store

(chorus)

You are always my God
You hear me all the time
You love me anyway
You make my life rhyme

Edit Draft Danger Hazardous

12/2/07 early Sunday 3:30 am (Thinking about what I'm hearing and wanting to write a very naughty song but I can't be sinful.)

(It's that screamer music, I forgot what it's called.)

Hazardous

(moderato)

Danger! Hazardous material
Danger! Marvelous, ethereal
Ranger, do you know what I mean
Ranger, do you know why I scream

(allegro)

You make me burn like a furnace
You keep me warm like a thermos
You make me melt like molten steel
Is this feeling real, is it real

(moderato)

> Danger! Don't come near me
> Danger! I see it clearly
> Ranger, how does that fire burn
> Ranger, do you want to learn

(largo)

> About heat, about fire
> About burning desire
> About passion?
> Applaud
> For God, for God, for God

Dear Brand New White Notebook,

Today, December 6, 2007, I got on an airplane with two suitcases full of whatever I thought was important and headed to see Jaz for the very first time in what was now thirty-six years. I didn't tell anybody that I was leaving ... not one soul. He said I can stay in a room in his house; it wasn't very big but it had a nice bed and a dresser. I was going to marry Jaziel Bachman. He didn't know that. He knew that. He must have known that. I am obviously still crazy.

12/6/07 3:45 On the airplane from Rome to Winnipeg, having left the snowy hills of New York. I see white vapor trails out the windows, one on each side.

Vapor Trails

> God is going ahead of me
> He has been this route
> Where no one understands
> Where there is no way out
>
> God is going ahead of us
> What is it we'll find
> I see Him on the right and left
> And I am not behind

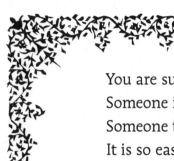

You are surrounding me Lord
Someone is praying for me
Someone that loves me Lord
It is so easy to see

(chorus)

Surround us Lord
With your Holy essence
Surround us Lord
We need your Holy presence

Dear Pinkie,

Jaz met me at the airport. I walked right by him. I guess I was expecting to see somebody with a head full of curly blond hair. I heard a man with a voice that I recognized, call out, "Alexa! Is that you?"

Edit Draft Sweet & Fruity

12/7/07 8:35 am

(country)

Sweet & Fruity

I'm a sinner
The worst of any saint
I wish I could be perfect
But I just simply cain't

I wish I could be like those Christians
Whose life is like a book
That reads from start to finish
Like a lesson that I took

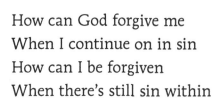

How can God forgive me
When I continue on in sin
How can I be forgiven
When there's still sin within

I've sinned against His Holy Name
I've sinned against the church
I've sinned against every friend
And left them in the lurch

There's no turning back right now
No way to pay the price
No way to make everything right
No way to make it nice

So only God can take it all
And turn it into beauty
Only God can lift it up
And make it sweet and fruity

Edit Draft Time Vapor

12/9/07 (Thirty-five five years can be a day in God's eyes.)

(contemplative R&B)

Time Vapor

Time is just a reason
For God to make a plan
Time is just a season
When God speaks to a man

Time is like a water
That fills an empty soul
With longing and desire
For love to make it whole

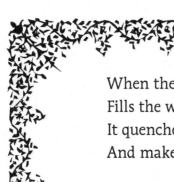

When the water's passion
Fills the well of life
It quenches every vessel
And makes the time so right

(chorus)
Time is like a vapor
That rises to the sky
And time is no longer
Now that you are mine

Edit Draft Holy, Sinless & Free

12/13/07 10 am Today this Bible verse was sent to me in an email from my good friend and wise Christian mentor, Signey Clark: "To him who is able to keep you from falling and to present you before his glorious presence without fault and with great joy--to the only God our Savior be glory, majesty, power and authority, through Jesus Christ our Lord, before all ages, now and forevermore!" Jude 24 NIV

(bright, powerful, joyful)

Holy Sinless and Free

All things are possible
For Him who is powerful
Who is able to keep even me
From falling to the depths of the sea

He'll give me as a present
To the God of creation
Holy, sinless and free
Holy, sinless and free

(chorus)

> This is how God will see me
> When given by grace
> With a smile on his face
> By the Savior who lives for me

Edit Draft Grace

12/13/07 11 am (A close relative of Jaz's, Grace, was born last night and so was this song with words by me and music by Jaz. Triple the interpretation: Jesus as a baby, any baby, God's grace. I think this would make a very nice Christmas carol.)

(lullaby)

Perfect Grace

Perfect Grace
Beautiful and sweet
Angel's breath
Cherub's feet

His perfect Grace
First revealed to me
His perfect grace
Now revealed to me

Miracle of life
Wonder of birth
Blessing of God
Unto the earth

Precious Grace
Lovely child
Born of God
Pure and mild

Edit Draft Hypocrite

12/20/07 1:30 Oswald "Our only priority must be to present Christ crucified ... What is important is for the worker's relationship to Christ to be strong and growing. His usefulness to God depends on that, and that alone.

I got an email from Sandra Dee. She wants to know why I "up and left" without telling anybody and why I got baptized at church.

I have no purpose now
My ministry is gone
I'm no use to anyone
Just put me in the ground
Look at that. I can't even write notes without meter. I'm hopeless.
(raucous then easy listening)

Hypocrite

Nothing I say means anything
I'm a horrible hypocrite
No one is listening anyway
I might as well just quit

Wait a minute
There was an old folk
Who gave a little smile
When I pushed her in the wheelchair
When we wheeled fast down the aisle

I think there was a child
Who needed just a lift
To reach the drinking fountain
And boost up just a bit

No none of that matters
I'm just not genuine
I can't pretend that who I am
Is really feeling fine

244

And maybe there is someone
Who needs a little help
Just to sweep the sidewalk
Or a smile for their self

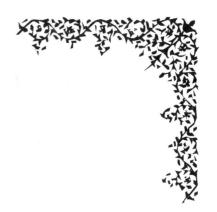

Hello Brilliant White Notebook,

12/22/2007

Two weeks after Jazzy Man met me at the Winnipeg Airport Arrival, we both went back to the Winnepeg Airport, got into an airplane, headed to Las Vegas and got married.

On the website of the Las Vegas Little White Wedding Chapel, you could point and click the date and time, wedding bouquet, limousine, and even choose minister or rabbi. You could even click to have Elvis perform the ceremony. Finally, this seemed to be a good thing to be clicking about.

It was the most beautiful wedding that ever was. One of Jaz's daughters and her husband flew to Las Vegas with us and stood up as witnesses. The little trailer was all decorated with artificial roses and they even had that stick-on stained glass on the patio door.

They had nine ministers on call at the Little White Wedding Chapel. They had assigned Pastor Bob for our 2 pm to 2:10 pm slot. He was eighty years old. He had performed about a million weddings and he knew what he was doing, to say the least. Well, that made one of us.

Very Private Gold Journal Notebook

12/27/07 Back in Winnepeg. At breakfast time, we were sitting in Jaz's house at the dining room table. We thanked God for bringing us together. Jaz took his guitar out of the case and started playing a beautiful melody that he made up right then and there. I spontaneously sung the words after I heard Jaz playing each verse on his guitar. This had to be some of the most fun I have ever had in my life!

I have landed into a life of love and peace and grace.

(slow & thoughtful)

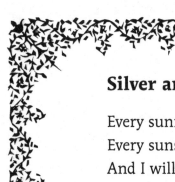

Silver and Gold/Our Journey

Every sunrise is made of silver
Every sunset is made of gold
And I will be with you forever
As our dreams unfold.

(chorus)

This is our journey
And this is our song
We will be together
As long as life is long

So bring the silver sunrise
Bring on the silver sun
Lift your hands at sunset
With a prayer that makes us one

Look to the heavens
Look up to the sky
Where hope and the future
Are ours now and when we die

12/27/07

Dearest White Notebook,

Back in Winnipeg, boxing up some of Jaz's old stuff, listening online to Brian Houston, Hillsong Church, Australia

I am contemplating the emptiness of our past marriages, our past goals, and thinking about the pleasure of loving the Lord and each other as our ordained destiny and that our musical work is a supernatural outpouring of love.

(style: Rhythm & Blues)

Empty Boxes

When my tears of past regret
Of lonely evenings spent
Trying to reclaim
Empty promises and fame
Begin to lose their hold
Their lifeless images of gold
Then I realize my only goal
My only pleasure
The only purpose of my soul
Is to be with you, Lord
To be with you

Empty promises
Vain pursuits
Empty boxes
Wrapped in truth

Your loving destiny
For my loving soul
Is all that matters
All that makes me whole

Edit Draft I'd Rather

12/29/07 Oswald Chambers: "When God gives you a vision you must walk in the light of that vision (1 John 1:7 If we walk in the light as he is in the light) Even though your mind and soul may be thrilled by it, if you don't walk in the light of it, you will sink to a level of bondage never envisioned by our Lord... When you find that one of your favorite and strongly held views clashes with the vision, don't begin to debate it. If you do, a sense of property and personal right will emerge in you--things on which Jesus placed no value..."

In Australia, mate means friend, but you can triple the interpretation: God, you, any friend.

Jaz and I go around to the different retirement centers and sing this for the lonely old people. We love doing this because it makes them and us feel great! They don't ask us any questions. They like whatever we sing. Most of the old people are pretty much deaf.

I'd Rather

    I've been all around this world
    Every tourist place and town
    From Mexico to Malibu
(some reflective notes)
    I'd rather be with you

    I'd rather just stay home
    Even talking on the phone
    Not Jamaica or Peru
(some reflective notes)
    I'd rather be with you

    I could dive I could swim
    I could fly I could fish
    I could ski the mountain trails
(some reflective notes)
    But I'd rather hear your tales

(chorus)

    Because you
    You are my great escape
    You take me places that are great
(some reflective notes)
    I'd rather be with you, my mate

Edit Draft Open

1/02/08 11 am (worshipping God in the dining window sunshine)

(slow and warm tones)
(soul)

Open Soul

When I enter into your presence
When I bathe in your caress
When the warmth of your love
Whispers I love you dear

Then I feel the touch of your heart
I know the depth of your love
I hear the sound of your breath
Whispering I love you near

I know your love, my God
I know the feel of your light
I know the sound of your breath
Filling the depths of my height

(chorus)

I feel your love God
I know your love is whole
And I love you so much God
For loving my open soul

Chapter 18

Gold Notebook,

1/5/08 10 am On the way to tour Grand Marais, Minnesota from Winnipeg. I notice that, in Canada, they pay a lot of attention to the environment. There are tall evergreens everywhere. There are recycling bins everywhere. Gen 12:8 NIV "Abram built an altar to the Lord and called on the name of the Lord."

Forest Nation

God this forest nation
Speaks of your creation
Where we pitch our tent of worship
And call upon your name

Where endless birches ripen
And blossom into lichen
With boundless crystal waters
Lapping at the rocky shore

When the wonder of your beauty
Enthralls my very soul
I know that you are lovely
As on your name I call

(chorus)

How lovely is your name, Lord
If all that our eyes see
Represents your beauty
In all its majesty

Edit Draft Unravel

1/7/08 6 am Luke 10:25, 27 NIV " ... what must I do to inherit eternal life?"

Unravel

You know how to wait, Lord
As I know you wait for me
From the dawn of man's creation
You knew what had to be

You waited for the perfect time
To send your son to earth
Waited for the very moment
That you would give him birth

You waited and you watched
As mankind floundered here
With very few that trusted
Not giving in to fear

(chorus)

Then you watched with pleasure
As one by one they came
To worship you through Jesus
When they called upon your name

And now you wait for me, Lord
As I struggle to unravel
The garment that does not quite fit
Into the suitcase of my travel

251

Edit Draft American Rights

1/08/08 6am I wake up with a new song. I am free to worship as loud as I like! Jaz gets out his guitar, plays along and tells me what notes I'm singing at 6am! What a guy!

(hard rock)

American Rights

6/4 time
B C B A G A G A
1/2 1/4 1/8 1/8 1/8 1/8,1/8 1/8
　　　My right as an A mer i can

B C B A
1/2 1/4 1/4 1/2
　　　My right is this

B C B A G A
1/2 1/4 1/4 1/8 1/8 1/4
　　　I have the right to find

B C B A A G G
1/2 1/8 1/8 1/8 1/8rest 1/8 1/8 1/8 1/8rest
　　　Life, Li ber ty, Hap pi ness

(repeat melody)
1/2 1/4 1/4 1/8 1/8 1/4
　　　Hold on to what you have

1/2 1/4 1/4 1/8 1/8 1/4
　　　Hold on if you are free

1/2 1/4 1/4 1/8 1/8 1/4
　　　Hold on to all your rights

1/2 1/4 1/4 1/8 1/8 1/8 1/8rest
　　　Hold on to Li ber ty

(Anthem)

B C F
1/4 1/4 whole
    Worship freeee

B C F
1/4 1/4 whole
    Worship freeee

B C B C
1/2 1/4 1/4 1/2
    Hold on my child

B C F F
1/4 1/4 whole 1/4
    Wor ship freeee ly

Edit Draft Vindication

1/16/08 2:30 pm (Jaz & I read Isaiah 54 while looking at the mountains around Thunder Bay, Ontario, where we're visiting his relatives. There is one called the Sleeping Giant that looks like an Indian taking a nap on Lake Superior.

(Even though those around us may be fearful, the promises of the Lord to us remain unchanged. He will protect, establish and instruct us and our children and give us peace.)

Isaiah 54:10-17 NIV

Vindication

    Though the mountains shake with fear
    And tremble in their footing
    You will not be shaken
    My promise is not breaking

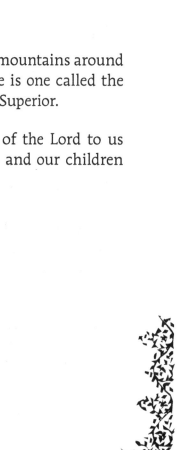

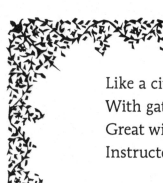

Like a city set on stone
With gates of precious rubies
Great will be your children's peace
Instructed by the Lord

Terror will not come near
It is I who raise up nations
No weapon formed against you
Will harm my prized creation

(chorus)

O, children of the Servant
Great is your heritage
O, Servants of the Lord
Great is your vindication

Edit Draft Vindication reply

I like this one, you get inspired by everything you read and cherish.

Love,
Jaz

Edit Draft Sleeping Giant

I pulled up some lyrics that I wrote last April when I was still at the Lodge. When I wrote this, I had no clue that they had a Sleeping Giant mountain in Thunder Bay, Ontario.

4/25/07 5 am (flowing onto the screen, triple interpretation)

(1 Sam 17:45-47)

Sleeping Giant

If he wants to lie sleeping
It doesn't matter at all
If he wants to be standing
Goliath will fall

If he wants to lie sleeping
Though the giant is tall
If he wants to be standing
Down he will fall

The problems, the issues
The portents of life
The what ifs and maybes
The products of strife

The questions, the answers
The when and the what
The could bees and should bees
The sting of distraught

Pick up your sling
Put in the stone
Find the forehead
Find its home

Find the place
Where bad thoughts live
Target the enemy
His push and give

Though you come against me
With sword and sharpened spear
In the name of the Lord Almighty
I come against you without fear

The God of the armies of Israel
The One the world will know
The battle is the Lord's
Into our hands you will go.

Edit Draft Apostles' Creed
1/18/08 4:30 pm (These things remain the same.)

(In the middle of the night, I heard the melody and the words, plunked it out on a little keyboard and jotted it down as best I could, all without waking up Jaz. Maybe he can sing this for the Canadian Indians.)

(congregational Indian chant, I found out that there are a lot of native Canadians in the Winnipeg area and all over Canada)

(every line is to be sung by leader and repeated by congregation/tribe/band)

(moderately fast tempo, major key)

Apostles Creed

I believe in God my Father
Who created heav'n and earth
And in peace in God the Father
In Jesus Christ of virgin birth

I believe God's Son is Jesus
Who was crucified and died
Who came back to life just for me
Who promised life and never lied

I believe He lives in heaven
Seated on His holy throne
I am there with all whom he loves
When His praises are my very own

256

I believe in His Holy Spirit
His communion with us here
I believe in His forgiveness
Forever life and without fear

Good Morning Lexie!

Oh yeah good stuff. Creed. I got the melody.

You're amazing!
Jaz

Edit Draft Liquid Gold

1/27/08 midnight:01 Song of Songs 8:7 NIV

Jaz said something like this to me but I didn't actually hear him. I wrote down what I did hear.

Liquid Gold

As the grave will not give up the dead
So my heart will hold you, Love, my love
And never surrender my precious love
Or give you up to the waters of dread

But I will forever and always hold
You in the highest region of regard
A precious treasure of precious love
That burns in my heart like melted gold

The blazing flame of whitest heat
Kindled by God's outstretched hand
Fire heated the purest, finest gold
Poured liquid gold into my heart

My heart holds you, made of gold
Never will I trade or give you away
You, Love, are the treasure of my heart
Precious gold burning until eternity

Edit Draft Second Birth

2/1/08 1 am. Jaz and I stayed up late and recalled our past rescues by the Holy Spirit from death by depression and our present joyful collaboration. I always write all the lyrics. He never even tries to change any of the words. I don't change any of his notes or chords. I wouldn't know how. Life is good.

Romans Chapters 6-8 NIV

(duet, operetta)

Second Birth

(bass voice)

> Am I a sinner or aren't I
> Everybody says that I am
> I guess my sins are obvious
> I'm an unholy man
>
> Well that's the way it is
> I'm a rotten sinner I guess
> I tried to do everything right
> But my life was a total mess

(soprano voice)

> I don't feel like a sinner
> I feel really happy inside
> I think the only thing that hurts
> Is my reputation and pride

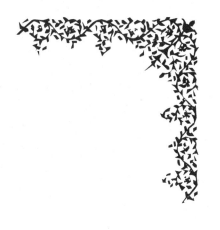

Have I hurt Christ by what I've done
Have I hurt my family or friends
Have I hurt the cause of Jesus
Is there no way to make amends?
I don't want to think about this

It makes my head just hurt
Getting everything back to right
Is a whole mess of a lot of work

Not only that, it's pointless
There's no way to get it back
No route back to square one
Short of a heart attack

(bass voice)

Might as well have killed me
There wasn't a reason to live
In the situation I was in
Something had to give

(soprano voice)

So in his love and mercy
God provided the way
The route for my liberation
Freedom in my day

Nobody seems to like that
They all think I should have stayed
And been a martyr for the cause
Been crucified in Christ's way

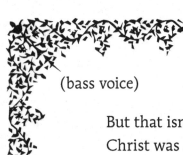

(bass voice)

> But that isn't what God wanted
> Christ was already crucified
> He doesn't need me to do the same
> When Christ already died

(soprano voice)

> So I'll enjoy my freedom
> And laugh and sing and play
> And revel in the forgiveness
> That Christ gave in his way

(bass voice)

> And when that day really comes
> When I'm no longer on this earth
> Then I'll hug the feet of Jesus
> And thank him for my second birth

Fresh Green Notebook

2/4/08 2 pm (While looking out the window of our little house in the city on Highland Street. It's a modest brick two story with an old wooden door. I'm eating a tuna fish sandwich.)

Mountain Cabin

> I'm in a mountain cabin
> Like Henry David Thoreau
> Soaking in the scenery
> The valley down below
>
> Breathing in the cold air
> The fire's woody smoke
> The sound of squirrels chirping
> The rustle of an oak

The evergreen's sweet fragrance
The sparkle of the snow
The solitude of God's creation
A space within my soul

Where God can work his wonder
The creation of his mind
And bring it forth for all to see
A work for all mankind

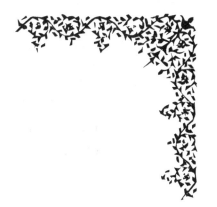

2/12/08 noon

We went to a Pow Wow held at the public school. They had a big drum in the middle with about six young men beating it. Everybody was dressed in full colorful regalia. They let us dance around in a circle with all the Natives. We just had regular clothes. Some of the women sang some solos. We couldn't understand the words but there was anguish in their voices.

We came home, sat at the dining room table and I wrote in the notebook after looking at Isaiah 23: 2, 3, 6-9, 19 (You, God, will keep him in perfect peace whose mind is stayed on You, because he trusts in You.)

Jaz picked up his guitar, started playing some fabulous chords that were in a way similar to the Indian solos and sang a melody. I started playing some long notes on my flute then beating a pan with a wooden spoon.

(For J to sing to the Canadian Indians, they call their tribes "Nations")

(strong minor key, good solid beat)

Holy Nation

(chorus)

Come in Holy Nation
The Gate is open
Come in Holy Nation
Righteous people
Through His salvation

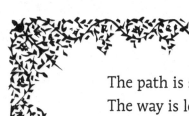

The path is smooth
The way is level
The way of truth
In all His Holy laws

(bridge: sweetly, no drum, add native flute)

My soul yearns for you in the night
In the morning my spirit wants you
When the fires rage upon the earth
Your people learn to trust in you
(rising)
The dead in You will live
Those in the dust of earth
They will wake and shout
They will have another birth

(chorus del cappa drum beat)

The gate is open
Come in Holy Nation
Righteous people
Through His salvation

Blue Notebook

3/26/08 9:30am Luke 16:19-31 NIV "The Rich Man and Lazarus"

We were praying for some of our unsaved relatives.

While sitting in our living room, Jaz read these lyrics that I had just written in my blue notebook. He immediately played a matching composition on his guitar.

(blues)

Lazarus

Lazarus do you hear me
You there by Abraham's side
How can I bridge the chasm
And get to the other side

I'm so parched and weary
And I only need a drink
Give me a crumb from your table
I cannot even think

Lazarus can you hear me
Can you come quickly to my aid
Can you save me from my torment
Before the price is paid

(chorus)

Can you save my brothers
Can you save my kin
Can you save my sisters
Before they're swallowed by their sin

Can you go to save my brothers
Can you warn them of my plight
Can you go to save them quickly
Before they're swallowed into night

3/26/08 10am
(blues)

So I Have To

What has happened to the sinner
Who walked on Abram's path
What will happen to the scholar
Will he find a love that lasts

What will happen to the poet
That walked on Dylan's road
What will happen to the sinner
Who cannot carry such a load

Will they find the love of Jesus
If I can't even find the chord
To bring them his salvation
The salvation of the Lord

Will they find the love of Jesus
If I can't even sing a song
That tells of Jesus steadfast love
Will they be searching all day long

(chorus)

So I have to tell the story
So I have to sing the song
I have to tell of Jesus' love
Even when I'm in the wrong (or) I have to sing it all day long

Edit Draft Save

3/26/08 10:30am (Maybe Jaz is supposed to sing this at a jail.)

(banjo, jailhouse rock)

Save Me

Give me that hellfire preachin'
That won't stand for any sin
Scare me back to reality
Don't let me harbor it within

Get me back to where I was
Where no sin could enter in
Get me back to the place of rest
Where there was no sufferin'

Give me peace in my spirit
Give me that place of rest
Where Jesus is my only love
Where only Jesus is the best

Save me from the pit of hell
Where I am looking for the light
Save me with your Holy arms
Don't let me stay in here all night

(chorus)

Save me, Jesus, save me
While you push away the fear
Save me, Jesus, save me
I want you to be near
I want you to be near

Sparkly Silver Notebook

4/6/08 Rick Barillo, a dear New York friend's husband, went home today. All of my New York church friends will be at the funeral.

I cannot afford to fly back for the funeral. All of Jaz's substantial savings went to his former spouse. The little bit that I managed to save is used up.

I did not receive any money or furniture in the divorce. Rich sold all the furniture and Lodge furnishings and spent the money. Coljens Lodge had to be short-sold, so there were no proceeds at all. Stephens Road lake house went back to the bank on foreclosure. Rich told the judge he had no income, so there is no alimony for me. He blamed that on the economy. He told his lawyer that people crashed all the airplanes and they were worthless. The businesses were bankrupt and he blamed that on me. He claimed that without me, there could be no construction, real estate or flight business. That part was true.

Jaz pays so much spousal support that his take-home pay wouldn't support a squirrel. Manitoba has a one size fits all formula for determining support. This is one case where legislation of generosity goes a little too far. Plus, they have further Canadian legislation, resulting in the mantra, "I didn't know taxes could be this high." Even when recited over and over again, in a monotone, nothing happens. Plus, I don't qualify yet for their health care and the fact that Canadian prescriptions are inexpensive turns out to be a myth. Who knew?

Until I can legally work in Canada, we are getting food from the Salvation Army. They have wonderful canned tuna. I found out what it feels like to be without basic necessities. It is frightening and humiliating. I volunteer at the Salvation Army in the Public Relations Department. I'm especially good at event planning and procuring donated prizes for people who participate.

Instead of going to Rick's funeral, I wrote a song, Jaz wrote the music and we sent a CD of Ricky to his wife.

(jazz, moderato, happy, with feeling)

Ricky

They're havin' a jazzy party in heaven
Because Ricky's made it there
They're havin' a jazzy party in heaven
And Ricky's without a care

He's singin' Hallelujah
With all the angel choirs
And jammin' with the great ones
From Satchmo to Fred Astair

He's singin Praise to Jesus
And dancin' down the street
To his mansion waitin' for him
Wavin' hello to all he meets

(chorus)

Oh Ricky's at the party
They made for him up there
And he is praising Jesus
And he's without a care

From: AlexaBachman@msn.com
To: rstonewall@sequoiachurch.ca
4/10/2008 0900:00

Hi Pastor Rusty,

Thanks for listening to some of our songs and our request to be part of the church worship team. We appreciate your leadership of the Music Ministry at Sequoia. I will try to answer some of your questions as best I can.

First, I don't write the songs or the lyrics. God writes them, I just write them down.

My background, spiritually speaking, is that I was saved when I was six. I have lots of personal experiences with God that I could share but that would take a book. I have had at least four near death experiences.

"Scarred" is about a time when I was nineteen and healed of a fatal blood disease, kind of like leukemia. At that time, I saw hell and an angel. I will send you the story of that.

I play clarinet. I sing but not on stage. I'm coming from an Assembly of God Church in New York. I played in the orchestra there. I played at the same high school as Jaziel Bachman, thirty-six years ago. He played trombone but as you know, he can play any instrument, primarily guitar. He has been doing Christian music ministry for about thirty years in various capacities, including travelling across Northern Canada with Spirit Alive Ministries.

I've been in Canada since Dec. 6th, 2007. We love Sequoia Church. There is a great Spirit of Acceptance amongst the people there.

About a year ago, January 2007, God told me, in a phenomenal way, that he wanted me to write lyrics. I had never written a lyric before in my life. In fact, I had written a play, based on the book of Esther that I had been trying to turn into a musical and had tried to write songs for it for over 10 years with no luck at all.

However, in January, I began to actually hear lyrics and write them down. The Spirit of God would come over me while I was awake or wake me while asleep and I would just write what I heard. Sometimes I don't know the meaning of some of the words and I have to look them up in the dictionary. One time, I thought someone turned the clock radio on and I tried, without success, to turn it off by tapping the snooze alarm! That song is called "Holy Altar". That same day, God gave Jaziel a vision that was the same as "Holy Altar." Sometimes I am singing a new song out loud, in my sleep that wakes me up.

I usually have an additional new song as I wake up every morning, with words and melody. To date, since January 2007, I have written down lyrics for about nine hundred songs. They are of every genre: Rock, Country, Bluegrass, Hip Hop, R&B, Motown, Jazz, Punk, Alternative Rock, etc. I've written a few of the melodies but I am not a composer. Jaz is composing and producing the songs as fast as he can.

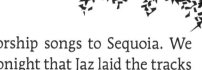

We would like to give as many of those that are worship songs to Sequoia. We should be able to send you a couple of worship songs tonight that Jaz laid the tracks for yesterday. Please don't feel obligated to use them, but feel free to use them if you choose.

I, seriously, am not sure what God is going have us do next with all this music, but I can't wait to find out. We appreciate your prayers for us.

IHS (In His Service),
Alexa Bachman

Chapter 19

Edit Draft Clear the Air

4/19/08 10 pm (J & I had a "discussion" after a particularly attractive teacher flirted with him at a party.)

(congregational worship)
(sparkling and fresh)

Clear the Air

I love the air after it rains
It smells so fresh and clean
All the dirt is washed away
The freshness of a dream

Clear the air
Wash away
All the dirt and shame
Clear the air
Wash my spirit
With your rain

All the hurt the pride the envy
The words I should not have said
Wash them with the love of God
Clear them from my head

Clear the air
Wash away
All the dirt and shame
Clear the air
Wash my spirit
With your rain

I love to smell the cleanness
Of the freshly fragrant air
When the Spirit rains upon us
Only your sweet love is there

Clear the air
Wash away
All the dirt and shame
Clear the air
Wash my spirit
With your rain

Edit Draft Diamond

4/30/08 noon (I don't hear a few words from Jaz as they are spoken but as a whole song of words from God to me)

(deliberately)
(style: Neil Diamond with a dance beat)

Diamond

You're my many sided diamond
Bril-i-ant and pure
Shining like the brightest star
My shining diamond is who you are

I love the young girl in you
The young girl dancing on the floor
Your smile shining as you dance
And you want to dance some more

I love the young girl in you
That delights in each new thing
A dew drenched flower on a stem
The sparkle on a diamond ring

I love you, you're my woman
You're my baby, you're my girl
You're my many sided diamond
There's none like you in this world

(chorus)

You're my diamond
You're my sweetheart
You're my darling, you're my gem
You're my lover and my friend

White Notebook

5/10/08 9 pm Mother's Day. I'm sad that I'm not with my kids but I suppose that if I were with them, I would never have had this song come to me.

(J and I are going to learn this song as a prayer for each other)

Ephesians 3:14-21 NIV

(with emotion and reverence)

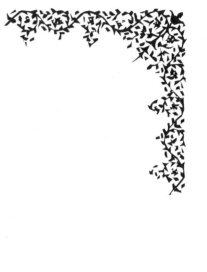

Ephesian Prayer

(intro)
I'm on my knees before the Father

In front of all angels and Christians as a whole
Praying that from his glorious treasures
He chooses to touch you with his power beyond measure
That you feel the power of his Spirit in your soul

That the Holy living God may live in your heart
That your faith will make Him a home
I pray that you, like a mighty oak rooted in a forest of love
May have the mighty power of God on His throne

And strengthened by His holy saints
May grab onto the hand of His Son
May you know the strength of this love that is
Granted by the power of the Holy One

Wider than the dark blue starry night
Longer than any road beyond horizon's line
Higher than any planet in the sky
Deeper than any ocean depth that you can find

May you be filled with God's infinite love
God who is able to do even more than we
Could ever think in our mind's eye to see
More than we could ever imagine could be

May God use His power to fill you
His power that gives us breath and life
For the glory of His living body
May you be alive in the power of Christ

For you and your children of every nation
Forever and ever alive in the power of Christ
For you and the children of every generation
Forever and ever alive in the power of Christ

Hello Red White and Blue Notebooks,

7/4/08 5:30pm Independence Day in New York ... in the whole US. Celebrations are going on, the same for Canada Day, too.

(After being invited and then disinvited to a party at a lake cottage not too far from Winnipeg, we drove to Seine River Trail and sat on a bench, by ourselves, by the river. Yes, Jaz's co-worker seriously said that they now did not have enough room for us at their party, after all. I guess everybody is entitled to control their own guest list.)

When something bad happens, I get the best lyrics!

(alternative)

When I Listen

When I listen to the river
That flows from Christ the rock
When I hear the flowing water
I hear my sweet Lord talk

I hear Him in the breezes
That flow among the trees
I hear him in the wind songs
That rush among the leaves

He speaks of love and mercy
In all that he provides
A river of contentment
A gentle flowing tide

I see Your love in all You've made
In all You've made for me
I see Your love in the river's flow
And as I walk among the trees

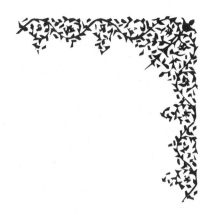

(chorus)

> God who made the river
> God who made the trees
> God who made all the earth
> Shows His love for you and me

Edit Draft Only A Man

7/27/08 Sunday 8:30 am (Pastor Rusty Stonewall, Music Minister, finally got back with Jaz about being on the worship team at church. He told J that he can't play guitar or sing on the church stage because he was divorced before we got married to each other. Same goes for me and my lyrics. I guess everybody is entitled to their own definition of sin.)

(I wrote these lyrics for J and he put a melody on it for himself to sing for nobody at church.)

(Cajun blues)

Only A Man

> I can't live up to people's
> Expectations
> I can't live down my
> Humiliation
>
> There's only so much
> That I can do
> The rest is up to you, o God
> The rest is up to you
>
> With what I've been through
> It's a wonder I'm alive
> With all I've been through
> It's a wonder I survived

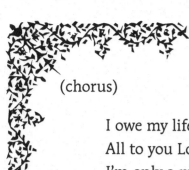

(chorus)

I owe my life and all I am
All to you Lord, all to you
I'm only a man
I owe my life and all I am
All to you Lord
All to you Lord
I'm only a man

Two Platinum Notebooks

8/4/08 11 am (I got the lyrics and Jaz got the melody with chords at Sequoia church, Sunday morning service. We were sitting in the middle. Both of us were writing in notebooks while Pastor Einstein was preaching on Job 38. I had my Bible open. Jaz heard the music. I heard words.)

Job 38:4-37 NIV

(contemporary)

Maker of Starlight

The morning stars sang together
The angels shouted, shouted for joy
The seas burst forth from their doors
When God formed the earth from its core

God gave orders to the morning
And showed the dawn its place
He pressed the mountains from the clay
And gave the earth its face

He entered the storehouse of the snow
The storehouse of the hail
He entered the heavenly room where
Lightening starts its trail

He cut a channel for torrents of rain
A path for the storm to spew
Rain for a blade in the desert sand
He waters the sand with dew

God gave birth to the morning frost
And iced the ocean's cap
He led the stars into their forms
Creating a stellar map

He endows the heart with wisdom
Gives understanding to the mind
He has the wisdom to count the clouds
He tips the water jars of the sky

(chorus)

Where were you, where was I
When God made the sky
The land, the birds, a fawn
Who am I compared to God
Maker of starlight, starlight and dawn

Spontaneous Human Combustion Sheet Music

Scarred

Lead Sheet

Lyrics by Alexa Colten

Music by Jaz Bachman

Heavy Blues
♩=74
A. Gtr.

My life did flow from His own blood_____ When I was weak and

near ly died_____ He sent His an gel_____ to my side to show He lives_____ all though He

died. The scars nev er go a way_____ It's the

strong est tis sue that's what they_____ say

scar tis sue of my veins_____ a re min der that He reigns_____ of

VIC TO RY IN HIS HO LY NAME OF VIC TO RY IN HIS HO LY NAME

NOW I'M AS STRONG AS TIS SUE SCARRED WITH HIS BLOOD IN SIDE MY VEINS

VEINS THAT HOLD THE STREAM ING PULSE OF VIC TO RY IN HIS HO LY NAME OF

LIV ING IN HIS HO LY NAME OF VIC TO RY IN HIS HO LY NAME OF

LIV ING IN HIS HO LY NAME.

Forever and Always

Alexa Coljen

Jaz Bachman

Holy Altar

2

Spontaneous Human Combustion

INSERT V.1 BETWEEN V.3 AND V.4

9

YOUR SONG

Voice

Alexa Colten

Jaz Bachman

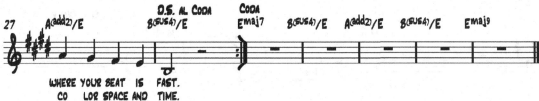

The most beau ti ful thing__ I've ev er seen__
I hear the strings The mus i cal things that

Pur ple gold and green and sound ing like wine__ The fruit of a rhyme that
Make the sea son bloom the pic tures of trees with flut ter ing leaves that

Chorus

came from you and me.
came from you and me.

I hear a brook a moun tain that shook a

Wind a bird a tree. I hear a star__ a beau ti ful chime a

Song a verse a rhyme.

Take me to__ the pas ture Lord take me
Take me where My tears are__ sweet__ the

To the blow ing grass. Take me to__ the sound of__ love__ take me
Riv ers made of wine. Take me__ where the pow'r of__ life__ lives in

Where your beat is fast.
Co lor space and time.

God With Us

Thunderous Voice
1st Chronicles 29:10-13

John Poniatowski

Voice

100 Rednecks and Me

Voice

Alexa Colten

Jaz Bachman

♩ = 120

C · · · · **F**

WAS THE SWEET EST DAY THERE WAS___ AND I WAS THERE BE CAUSE

5 **G** **C**

THEY WERE HAV ING AN AUC TION___ OF EV ERY KIND OF GUN

9 V.2 **C** **F**

THERE WAS A BON FIRE___ BLA ZIN' AND RAIN IN IT WAS HARD___ THE

14 **G** **C** Chorus

MEN WERE THICK AND SMELL IN IN THAT SMOKE Y SAND IT'S YARD THE

19 **C** **F**

AUC TION WENT FOR EV___ ER I WAIT ED THERE ALL DAY___ TO GET THAT

23 **G** **C**

FOR TY ONE JOHN SON I NEED THAT LORD I___ PRAYED. THE

28 **F** **C**

SWEET EST DAY THAT THERE___ COULD BE. BID DIN ON A

32 **G** **C**

JOHN SON A HUN DRED RED NECKS A ND ME.

Temple
Romans 8:38-39

Voice

Alexa Coljen

Jaz Bachman

Je sus in his ho ly tem ple his

spir it makes me whole. And though a moun tain shat ters it can't di vide my soul.

Not a tow er ing in fer no or depths of wid est girth not

death from hell or an y foe or life up on this earth. Not time or space or

de mons or a ny e vil power that roams the land and takes a stand a

gainst me an y hour. Will e ver sep a rate us will e ver drive a wedge.

Will e ver come be tween us or

Push us to the edge.

VOICE

PERFECT GRACE

Alexa Coljen

Jaz Bachman

Silver and Gold

Alexa Coljen

Jaz Bachman

Am G F G F Am
6 Am G/B C G Am G/B C
Ev ery sun rise is made of sil__ ver
Ev ery sun set is made of
12 D(add2) Fmaj7 G Am Fmaj7
Gold. and I will be with you__ for ev__ er
As our
19 G/B Am Am G F G F
dreams un fold
24 Am C C
this
29 G/B Am C G/B Fmaj7
is______ our jour ney_
and this______ is our song
36 C G/B Am Fmaj7 G(add2) A(add2)
we will be________ to ge ther
as long as life is long
42 A(add2) G(add2) A(add2) G(add2) Fmaj7 G(add2) A(add2) A(add2) G(add2) A(add2) G(add2)
as long as life is long.
as

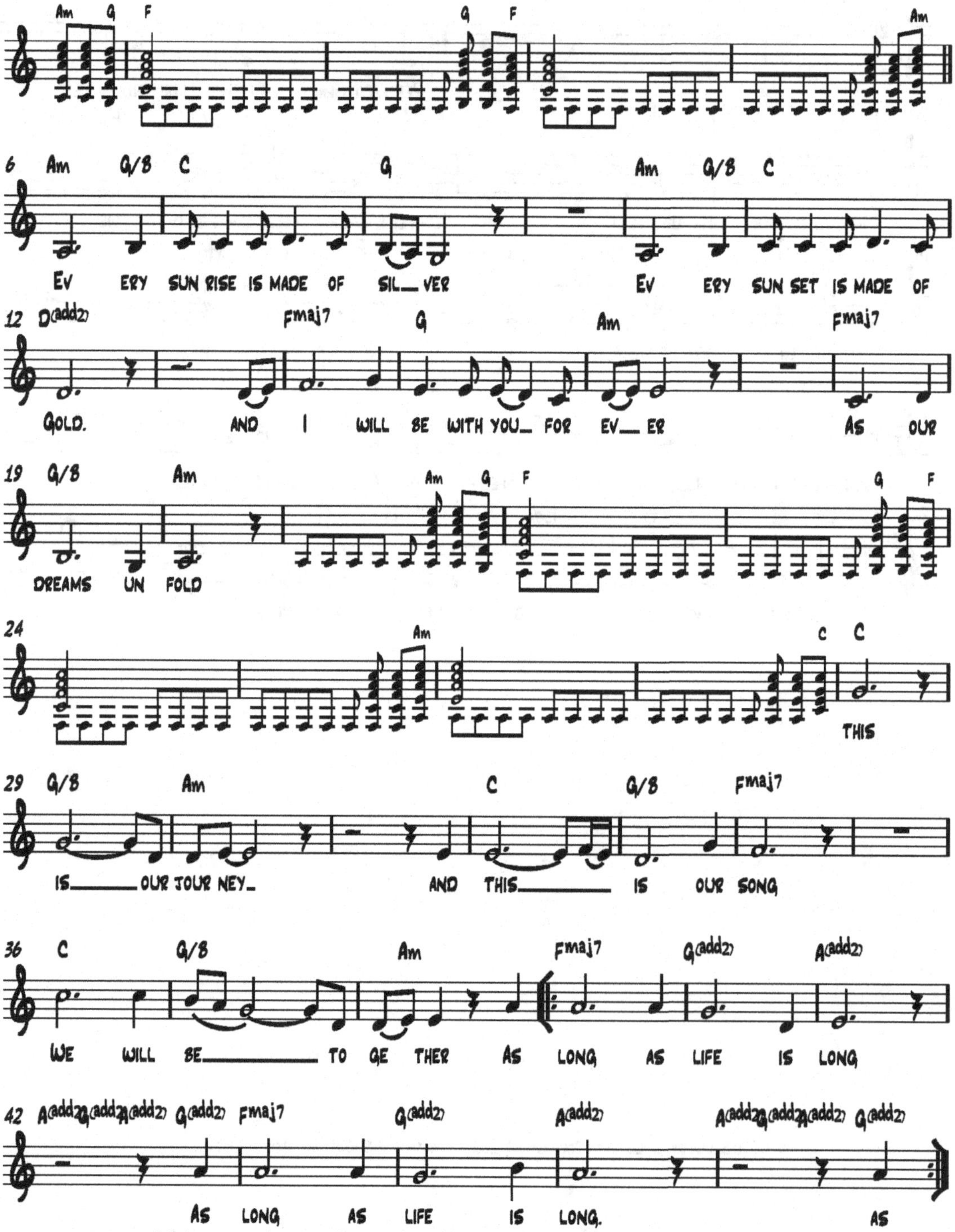

I'd Rather

Voice

Alexa Colten

Jaz Bachman

I'VE BEEN ALL A ROUND THIS WORLD___ EV ERY TOUR IST PLACE AND TOWN___ FROM
RA THER JUST STAY HOME___ E VEN TALK ING ON THE PHONE___ NOT JA

(SOME REFLECTIVE NOTES)

MEX I CO TO MAL I BU   I'D___ RA THER BE WITH YOU.
MAI CA OR PE RU

I'D   I COULD DIVE, I COULD SWIM, I COULD FLY, I COULD FISH, I COULD

(SOME MORE REFLECTIVE NOTES)

SKI THE MOUN TAIN TRAILS__   BUT I'D RATH ER HEAR YOUR TALES

BE CAUSE YOU   YOU ARE   MY GREAT ES CAPE   YOU TAKE ME

(NICE TO SEE THAT YOU'RE CATCHIN' ON)

PLA CES THAT ARE GREAT   I'D RA THER BE WITH YOU MY MATE___

American Rights

Voice

Alexa Colten

Alexa Colten

♩ = 100

My right as an Am er i can   My right is this   I have the right to find

Life   Li ber ty   Hap pi ness.   Hold   on   to what you have   Hold   on if

You are free   Hold   on   to   all your rights   Hold   on   to   li ber ty.

Wor ship Free   Wor ship free   Hold   on   my

Child   Wor ship free   ly

Apostles Creed

Alexa Colten

Jaz Bachman

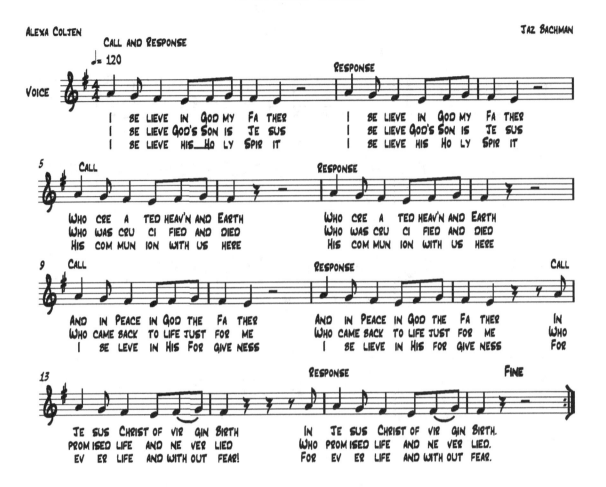

Lead Vocals

Holy Nation
Isaiah 23:2,3,6-9,19

Alexa Colten

Jaz Bachman

♩=100

Come in Ho ly na tion the gate is o pen

Come in right eous peo ple through his sal va tion

The path is smooth the way is lev el___ The way of truth in all his ho ly laws___ My

Soul yearns for you in the night in the Morn ing my spir it wants you. When the

Lazarus
Luke 16:19-31

Lyrics

Alexa Coljen

Jaz Bachman

Laz'rus do you hear me? You there by Ab ra ham's side. How can I bridge the chasm,

And get to the oth er side? I'm so parched and wear y and I on ly need a drink

give me a crumbs from your table I can not e ven think_____

Laz' rus can you hear me? Can you come quick ly to my aid? Can you save me from my tor ment

be fore the price is paid_____ Can you save my broth ers_

Can you save my kin Can you save my sis ters___

VOICE

Ricky's Song

Voice

Alexa Colten

Jaz Bachman

They're

HAV IN' A JAZ ZY PAR TY IN HEAV EN 'CAUSE RICK Y'S MADE IT THERE. They're

HAV IN' A JAZZ Y PAR TY IN HEAV EN CAUSE RICK Y'S WITH OUT A CARE. He's

SING IN HA LE LU JAH! WITH ALL THE AN GEL CHOIRS AND

JAM MIN' WITH THE GREAT ONES FROM SATCH MO TO FRED A STAIR.

WHEN I LISTEN

VOICE

Alexa Coljen

Jaz Bachman

2

G/D   D   G/D   D

HE___
I SEE

B D   G/B   D   G/B

SPEAKS OF__ LOVE AND__ MER_____ CY__   IN__ ALL THAT HE__ PRO_ VIDES__   A
YOUR LOVE IN__ ALL__ YOU'VE MADE__   IN__ ALL YOU'VE MADE FOR__ ME__   I SEE

D   G/B   C(ADD2) G/B   D   1. G/B

RIV ER__ OF__ CON TENT__ MENT   A__ GEN TLE__ FLOW ING__ TIDE.
YOUR LOVE IN THE__FLOW ING RI VER   AS I WALK A_____MONG THE__ TREES   I SEE

2. C(ADD2)   G/B   C(ADD2)

GOD WHO MADE THE RI VER__   GOD WHO MADE THE TREES__   GOD WHO MADE

C(ADD2)   G/B   D   G/D

ALL THE EARTH SHOWS HIS LOVE FOR__ YOU__ AND ME__

D   G/D   D

Only A Man

Alexa Colten

Jaz Bachman

ON LY SO MUCH__ THAT I CAN DO__ THE REST IS UP TO
OWE MY LIFE_____ AND ALL I AM__ ALL TO YOU LORD ALL

YOU O GOD THE REST IS UP TO YOU____
TO YOU LORD I'M ON__LY A MAN__

YOU____ THE REST IS UP TO YOU__ .

29

Maker of Starlight
Job 38:4-37

Alexa Coljen

Jaz Bachman

The morn ing stars sang to geth er   the an gels shout ed for joy   the

Seas burst forth from their doors   when God formed the earth from its core

God gave or ders to the mor ning   and showed the dawn its place   He

Pressed the moun tains from the clay   and gave the earth its face   He

En tered the store house of the snow   the store house of the hail   He

En tered the heav ven ly store room   where light ening starts its trail   He

Cut a chan nel for tor rents of rain   a path for the storm to spew

Rain for a blade in the des sert sand   He wat ers the sand with dew